The Shortchanged: Women and Minorities in Banking

The Shortchanged:
Women and Minorities in Banking

written and researched by

Rodney Alexander

and

Elisabeth Sapery

of

The Council on Economic Priorities

DUNELLEN PUBLISHING COMPANY, INC.
386 Park Avenue South, New York, New York 10016

COUNCIL STAFF

The Council on Economic Priorities is a non-profit organization established to disseminate unbiased and detailed information on the practices of U.S. corporations in five major areas: employment, environmental quality, military production, political influence, and foreign activities.

The Council presents this information in the belief that these practices have a profound impact on the quality of American life. The American public should be aware of this impact in order to assure corporate social responsibility.

Contents

Preface and Acknowledgments

In the boardrooms of major corporations, decisions are made daily
that can profoundly affect the quality of life in the U.S.: decisions
on how environmental problems are to be handled may determine how clean
our air and water remain; others regarding opportunities for employment
and upgrading of minority group members and women may affect their
ability to become wholly integrated into society; decisions on the goods
to be supplied to the Department of Defense may determine the extent of
our military commitments; decisions regarding the conduct of overseas
operations may affect the lives of foreign nationals and the image of
the U.S. abroad.

The Council on Economic Priorities was formed in 1969 to analyze such
decisions, to evaluate the practices of individual corporations, and
to determine which companies have the most responsible records.

The Council's research findings are published in bi-monthly Economic
Priorities Reports as well as in longer in-depth studies which are now
read regularly by over 3,000 subscribers. (See back page for subscrip-
tion information.)

With such information, concerned Americans can assess the impact of
corporations on their own lives, and can express their approval or
criticism of corporate policies and practices as shareholders, students,
businessmen, consumers, and citizens.

SHORTCHANGED is the Council's first in-depth study in the employment
area. While it was written by a team of Council writers, the research
for the study could not have been compiled or adequately evaluated without the help of many members of the banking industry, state and Federal
government officials, feminist and minority groups, and technical
experts on the problems of employment and minority economic development.

We are also deeply indebted to Pat King, Beverly Wadsworth, Susan Davis,
Molly D'Esposito, Phyllis Hager, Sharon Pierce, Marsha King, Barbara
Phillips, Joan Baeder, June Inglena, and the placement bureaus of Beaver,
Connecticut, and Barnard Colleges for their valuable insights and contacts
into women's issues. Special thanks also to Leslie Allan, George Riggs,
Stan Strachen, Denis Alee, Edward Riegelhaupt, Father Theodore Purcell,
Garland C. Guice, Consuelo Miller, Otis T. Streeter, Milton Davis, Peter
McNeish, Patricia RobertsHarris, William Hudgins, Arthur Ziegler,
William Turner, Deighton Edwards, Mike Iovenko, Nancy Lane, Tom Jones,
and Don Alexander. Deep thanks go to Louise Skow for typing the final
manuscript; to all the members of the Council for their continuous help
and encouragement; and to Pat Carbine, Joanne Edgar, and Ms. magazine

for providing us with the title and other aid. This project would
not have been possible without the assistance of all those employees
at the sample banks who commented freely and honestly on their
respective institutions but who must remain anonymous.

Wellesley and Bryn Mawr Colleges were most helpful in interesting
student interns in working with us.

Finally, we are particularly thankful to the Playboy Foundation for
a grant toward the part of the study dealing with women.

Foreword

"The public be damned"

"The public," said William Vanderbilt, in an outburst that has lingered much longer than he would have wished, "be damned." He was talking, of course, in another age, when the prevailing ethic of the business community was that the public existed for the convenience of business, rather than the other way around.

Nowadays no businessman would dare say that the public should be damned, or even disregarded. And yet, as Shortchanged, a study of discrimination in the banking industry reveals, the public is still damned in at least two respects:

First, many businesses believe that the public has no "right" to poke around investigating its social conduct, asking awkward questions, such as what its recruiting or promotion policies are with respect to minority groups and women.

Second, there is ample evidence that the public is being damned because discriminatory practices prevent minority groups and women from achieving economic success on equal terms with whites and males.

This pioneering study of the banking industry analyzes and documents these social failures of the banking industry in detail. But the study is important beyond the significant facts that it discloses. Perhaps more clearly than any previous C.E.P. investigation, it highlights the difference between two business philosophies--the old view that business is, in a social as well as a legal sense, a _private_ preserve into which the public has no right to look, much less enter; and the newer view that however private its ownership, business is inextricably a part of a larger society, to which it owes a full and candid report on practices and activities that have important repercussions on our national life.

Happily, as this report by the Council on Economic Priorities shows, a few of our biggest banks recognize this unavoidable social aspect of their business activities, try hard to improve their performance in critical social areas, and are not afraid to tell the public what they have done or mostly have not done. Unhappily, as SHORTCHANGED also shows, many of the banks studied still take the view that what goes on in their offices is nobody's business but their own--surely as scandalous a disrespect of society's rights as that displayed by any Vanderbilt.

In SHORTCHANGED: Minorities and Women in Commercial Banking, as in its previous studies of the paper industry and the utilities, the C.E.P. does not seek to act as a self-appointed guardian of the public morality. It tries hard to avoid both praise and blame with regard to its findings, merely reporting the facts as best it can ascertain them. The Council wants nothing more than that the public should be informed, as fully as is compatible with the acknowledged right of companies to protect their legitimate business secrets.

In examining hitherto "private" areas of banking practice, the C.E.P. has thrown important light on one area of social responsibility, employment practices, of the American banking system. Through this window the public can look in and if it wishes, take action--switching its accounts from one bank to another, urging the stricter enforcement of existing legislation, or endorsing new social legislation. More important, now that the shutters have been thrown open, perhaps the bankers will look out and recognize that their attitudes of secrecy are uncomfortably close to those of William Vanderbilt. Let those who deny the public's right to know remember that private enterprise exists not by the word of God but by the chartered consent of the public, acting through its government. Let us hope that a word to the wise will be sufficient.

Robert L. Heilbroner

The Shortchanged: Women and Minorities in Banking

Part 1

Summary of Findings

The Council on Economic Priorities has found:

---that employment discrimination against minorities and women is endemic to commercial banking;

---that a majority of the commercial banks studied are unwilling to permit public scrutiny of their employment and minority lending practices; and

---that both the secrecy and the discrimination are perpetuated by Federal law, policy and complacency.

More specifically, the C.E.P. has ascertained the following:

1.) <u>Minorities</u>: In five of the six cities studied*, minorities are employed at levels 18 to 38 percentage points below their share of the local labor forces; in New York, however, black and Hispanic American employment exceeds labor force representation by almost five percentage points. Minorities constitute 25% of all employees in the sample, but they are primarily restricted to office and clerical, blue collar and service jobs. Only 9% of all professional , technicians and sales workers, and 6% of all officials and managers in the sample are minority group members. Their share of the latter category in the three-bank aggregates** ranges from 8% of all executives in New York, to under 1% in Atlanta.

2.) <u>Women</u>: A majority of employees in the sample, and the majority in the entire industry, are women, and women are employed at levels exceeding their share of the local labor force in all of the six cities studied. But they are overwhelmingly concentrated in low-level, poorly-paid work that offers little opportunity for advancement. Nearly 73% of all office and clerical jobs at the 18-bank sample are held by women. They hold just 15% of all official-managerial positions in the sample. Most of these women are white. In the three-bank aggregates, women's share of executive-level positions ranges from 19% in Detroit to just 4% in Philadelphia.

---

* Atlanta, Chicago, Detroit, New York, Philadelphia and Washington, D.C.
** Aggregate of statistics reported to the E.E.O.C. by the three largest banks in each city.

3.) <u>Probability</u>: The probability that an employee of a given race and sex will be found in a particular job category follows:

PROBABILITY OF EMPLOYMENT IN VARIOUS CATEGORIES
BY RACE AND SEX
18 Sample Banks

OFFICIALS AND MANAGERS:

White Males	Minority Males	White Females	Minority Females
1/3	1/12	1/17	1/48

PROFESSIONALS, TECHNICIANS & SALESWORKERS:

White Males	Minority Males	White Females	Minority Females
1/5	1/13	1/18	1/67

OFFICE AND CLERICAL:

Minority Females	White Females	Minority Males	White Males
1/1	1/1	1/1	1/3

BLUE COLLAR AND SERVICE WORKERS:

Minority Males	White Males	White Females	Minority Females
1/8	1/16	1/67	1/77

4.) <u>Correlation</u>: In CEP's sample there is no significant correlation between female and minority employment statistics and (a) the size of an individual bank; (b) percentages of women and minorities in the city labor force; or (c) percentages of women and minorities in the city population.

5.) <u>Performance of Individual Reporting Banks</u>: In general, existing patterns for the three-bank aggregates also apply to the individual reporting banks. Overall, the two New York banks, Manufacturers Hanover and Chase, have the best records with regard to minorities, hiring them at levels commensurate with their representation in the city work force, and placing them in executive positions in greater proportions than any other reporting banks. Citizens & Southern and National Bank of Washington have the poorest records: they hire minorities at levels well below their representation in the city work force, and have the smallest minority representation in executive positions.

4

Women do not fare significantly better. They constitute approximately 70% of all office and clerical workers at the reporting banks; however, they are not represented in professional, technician, and sales or in official and managerial jobs in similarly large numbers. Generally, all of the reporting banks hire women in proportions exceeding their share of the city labor force. For executive positions, however, Manufacturers Hanover has the best record (25% of its officials and managers are females) while First Pennsylvania has the worst (6%).

6.) Cooperation, Resistance and Their Implications: This is the first C.E.P. study to encounter massive resistance from a majority of the corporations under review. The uncooperativeness of most sample banks was the key obstacle to C.E.P.'s efforts to evaluate their practices. Seven banks provided a reasonable amount of data; six provided partial data; and five declined to provide any. Inherent in this uncooperativeness are grave implications regarding institutions which enjoy power without accountabilty.

7.) Changing the Status Quo: No substantial improvement in the proportion of women and minorities in high-level jobs can result if the industry's present programs continue. This conclusion stems from data on: first-time promotions to officer; composition of executive-management training programs; distribution of minority and female executives; and the policies of three industry associations.

8.) The Role of Government: Existing laws regarding fair employment are adequate, but enforcement by the Treasury Department is not. The department has never denied Federal funds to any major bank for non-compliance, although C.E.P. found extensive and unmistakable employment bias at many such institutions. The department's attitude appears complacent. Treasury, the chief enforcement agency for commercial banking, does not publish the names of banks reviewed, does not publish the results of reviews, and claims that it keeps no records of banks which fail to comply.

9.) Minority Lending: Evidence obtained was insufficient to permit comprehensive evaluation of individual banks' minority lending activities The banks often refused to supply data, and a number of them made the novel claim that they themselves were not sure what they were doing in that area.

A more complete description of C.E.P.'s findings appears on page 154.

5

Banking, Minorities, and Women

The Importance of Commercial Banking

In terms of economic leverage and employment capacity, commercial banking is plainly one of this country's most important industries. It is the major source of short-term funding and a major source of white-collar jobs, employing almost 970,000 people as of March 1971.[1] In addition, 44 of the 50 largest banks in the United States are located in the 50 cities with the country's highest concentrations of black population, and Federal and state regulations prevent many of these institutions from joining the exodus to suburbia.

Wright Patman, Chairman of the House Committee on Banking and Currency, has spoken of the industry's power and the manner in which that power is used:

> Make no mistake about it, the banking institutions are powerful. I do not underestimate their strength. I have seen it in the halls of Congress. I well know that most public officials hesitate to step on the toes of an influential and powerful banker. This has given the average banker an inflated opinion of just how far he can go before the American public blows the whistle. The banks operate pretty much on the theory that public opinion doesn't count. In my opinion, they are fooling themselves on this score. The banking community could do wonders if it would abandon its robber baron philosophy. It could help build schools and housing; it could help provide the money needed to wipe out pollution; with its practically unlimited resources and power, it could be the greatest source for good.[2]

And a survey titled "Community Opinion Leaders' Views of Banks and Bankers," taken by Louis Harris Associates in 1970, contained this summary:

> Banks appear to be facing something of a challenge in the community social sphere. There is overwhelming feeling that exercising leadership in community problems is the legitimate realm of bankers, and there is widespread feeling that bankers are among the most public-spirited citizens of the community. However, under close scrutiny, the effectiveness of bankers' efforts in the community area appears subject to some question, particularly in the areas of racial problems, helping the needy, and pollution. Bankers have the mandate...they are expected to exercise real leadership on a broad scale. Up to now, the leaders do not feel it has been done well.[3]

7

Banks' proximity to black communities has stimulated criticism of their minority lending practices. One member of the Federal Reserve Board has charged banks with contributing to ghetto problems by refusing to lend money to inner city projects. Minority employment practices are questionable, too. In 1970, members of minority groups accounted for 13.7% of the U.S. labor force,[4] and 3.6% of the officials and managers in all white collar industries, but only 2.7% of the officials and managers at banks. In 1960, the nation's 14,000 commercial banks employed fewer than one black apiece. By 1969, they employed nearly 50,000--at least three times as many--but despite this improvement at the entry level only about 1,000 blacks were executives.

For many years, a majority of bank employees have been females; the figure for 1970 was 61%. And more women are executives in banking than in any other industry. Yet only 10% of banking's officers are female, and most of that 10% hold jobs in the lower end of the category, like assistant cashier.

According to an Equal Employment Opportunity Commission report published in January 1971, "greater than nine of every ten women [in banking] were situated in clerical jobs, compared to fewer than four of every ten women in all industries."[5] Therefore, while women encounter fewer problems than minorities when seeking employment in banking, the work is likely to be low-level and the chances for advancement poor.

This pattern of bias cannot be altered without substantial changes in attitudes. One personnel specialist has written: "Cliches [about employment of women] are usually one part truth and nine parts nonsense, but they are difficult to uproot."[6] According to folklore, women work outside the home only to find husbands and, having found them, leave their jobs without a backward glance. In fact, as of March 1970, 66% or 20.7 million of the 31 million women in the labor force worked to support themselves or their families,[7] and unnumbered women have left their jobs when pregnant only at employers' insistance. Another bromide, that females have higher rates of absenteeism and turnover, is refuted by a Labor Department statement that "women workers have favorable records of attendance and turnover when compared with men employed at similar job levels and under similar circumstances."[8] Nevertheless, solemn nonsense about women workers is still commonly cited. Women are said to be unable to travel because they cannot eat meals alone in a hotel; to be too emotional to take criticism; and to be unable to entertain male customers because they cannot pick up a restaurant check.

Minority women encounter magnified problems. The author of "Job Discrimination and the Black Women," Sonia Pressman, has written:

> Civil rights is one of the principal issues facing the country today--if not the principal issue. But when most people talk about civil rights, they mean the rights of black people. And when they talk about the rights of black people, they generally mean the rights of black males.[9]

Black women generally earn less than either white women or black men and are more likely than the other two groups to be unemployed. In Ms. Pressman's words, the black woman "has a significant amount of family responsibility and economic need and a lower income than the black male or the white female."[10]

In sum, during a period when more and more city dwellers are members of racial minorities and when national discussion of the status of women has increased, the urban location and economic power of the banking industry have made it a logical focal point for minorities and women seeking employment opportunities and economic development.

Notes

[1] *County Business Patterns, 1971*, U.S. Department of Commerce, CBP-71-1.

[2] Remarks of the Honorable Wright Patman, Chairman, House Banking and Currency Committee, to the Public Affairs Forum, Harvard Business School, February 9, 1970.

[3] Louis Harris Associates, Inc., *Community Opinion Leaders' Views of Banks and Bankers in 1970*, Vol. II, p. 134.

[4] U.S. Department of Commerce, Bureau of the Census, telephone interview, October 1972.

[5] Martha Rogers, *Employment of Minorities and Women in Commercial Banking* (Washington: Equal Employment Opportunity Commission, Office of Research,1971), p.2.

[6] Ray A. Killian, *The Working Woman: A Male Manager's View* (New York: American Management Association,1971), p.106.

[7] "Why Women Work" (Washington: U.S. Department of Labor, Employment Standards Administration, Women's Bureau,1971) , N.WB-3092.

[8] *Facts About Women's Adsenteeism and Labor Turnover* (Washington: U.S. Department of Labor, Wage and Labor Standards Administration, Women's Bureau, August 1969), p.1.

[9] Sonia Pressman, "Job Discrimination and the Black Woman" (no place of publication mentioned: March 1970), p. 103.

[10] *Ibid.*, p.104.

Scope and Method

Uniqueness

This study is the first known attempt by a private, independent research organization to provide the public with comparative information on banks' minority and female employment practices and minority lending activities and to do so without promising the banks anonymity in return for their cooperation.

In recent years, three other studies have dealt with, or touched on, the same area. The Negro in the Banking Industry was published in 1970; its author is Armand J. Thieblot, Jr., assistant professor of management at the College of Business and Public Administration of the University of Maryland. This scholarly work provided historical and legal perspective on blacks' entry into the industry and presented statistics on 46 large banks in all parts of the country. New Workers in the Banking Industry: A Minority Report by Dr. R. David Corwin appeared the same year. This study, which was funded by the U.S. Department of Labor, looked at circumstances surrounding the influx of Negroes and other racial minorities into six major New York City banks. And a Ralph Nader task force headed by David Leinsdorf studied the activities of New York's First National City Bank in a 1971 report titled Citibank.

Neither the Thieblot nor Corwin studies identified the participating institutions by name. The Leinsdorf project was not specifically concerned with employment of women and minorities. None of the three dealt with bank involvement in minority economic development.

Purposes

C.E.P. has attempted to ascertain whether a statistical pattern of discrimination exists at 18 commercial banks. To make this determination the Council asked:

---How many members of each racial and sexual group are employed in the commercial banking industry at the three largest banks in each of six cities and at 18 individual banks;

---How the employment levels of each racial and sexual group at these banks compare with the groups' representation in the local (city) labor force;

---How various racial and sexual groups of bank employees compare in regard to their representation in each job category--especially the official-managerial category---and in commercial lending; and

11

---What the probability is that an employee of a given racial or sexual group will work at each job level .

In addition, the Council sought to learn:

---What attempts have been made, and are being made, by banks, trade associations, and government to correct any inequities which may exist;

---Whether the performance of banks in providing equal employment opportunities varies with bank size and the composition of the local labor force;

---The extent to which the commercial banks in the sample are encouraging minority economic development; and

---The willingness of individual banks to disclose employment statistics and to discuss their employment programs and records fully and openly.

Labor force, rather than population, was considered because it excluded children and others who are not potential bank employees; city rather than national, labor force statistics were chosen because banks tend to recruit at the local level.

Definitions

The U.S. Government Public Information Office defines a "minority" person as a "person who is a member of a group which is under-represented in the total population." The great majority of the people covered by the term "minority" are black, with a smaller number of Hispanic Americans. Orientals and American Indians represent only about 1.0% of the minority employees in the C.E.P. sample.

"Minority economic development" is the effort to foster the growth of minority-owned businesses. In the banking industry, it has taken the form of "relaxed" credit standards, usually coupled with loan guarantees obtained through the Small Business Administration.

Areas Outside the Study

No attempt was made to compare banking with other industries because the nature of its jobs and "products" are not analogous to those in other industries included in Department of Commerce statistics.

While a number of banks participate in projects of a socially responsible nature--e.g. by sponsoring scholarships and community activities--these projects are not included in the study because they are not indispensable to a bank's survival, as are the labor of its employees and the making of loans. Another area, that of low- and middle-income housing, is so greatly affected by the policies of institutions like insurance companies and savings and loan associations that it cannot reasonably by examined solely in light of the activities of commercial banks.

Certain kinds of job discrimination, like those involving Jews, Italian-Americans, and the middle-aged and elderly, are not included, either because banks are not required to provide the Equal Employment Opportunity Commission with data on them or because investigations of the problems have recently been conducted by other organizations. And although exclusionary membership policies of some social clubs can reinforce an industry's tendency to draw its executives from an inbred milieu, thereby perpetuating existing inequities, the employment level seems to be the most effective way of breaking the cycle of discrimination.

Finally, female economic development is not covered. Government officials and bank executives have often stressed the strides supposedly made in minority employment and lending; and some statements have been made about the importance of placing women in responsible jobs in the industry. But little rhetoric and no regulation has yet been devoted to the subject of loans to female-owned businesses. Criticism of sexist discrimination in the granting of retail and commercial credit, however, has begun.* Plainly, more will follow.

Staff

The staff of the study consisted of two project directors, four summer student interns, and four outside consultants. One of the directors, a black man, was formerly an assistant project director for the East Harlem Triangle, an economic and sociological survey funded by the U.S. Department of Housing and Urban Development; he was also a former research associate at the Center for Urban Education. The other director, a white woman, is a former bank analyst for Blyth-Eastman Dillon. The consultants were: a publisher who specializes in minority economic development and banking; a professor of business and finance; a reporter for the _American Banker_; and a former management consultant for Arthur D. Little who holds a master's degree in social psychology.

Sample Selection

In May 1971, the Council on Economic Priorities selected a sample consisting of the three largest commercial banks, by total assets, in six cities. Five of the cities--New York, Chicago, Detroit, Philadelphia, and Washington--rank highest in the United States in black population. The sixth, Atlanta, ranks eleventh in the nation but was chosen because it adds geographical breadth to the study and because it has both a substantial black middle class and a reservoir of potential bank employees in the form of a large population of black college students. The banks, their deposits, and the size of their work forces are listed below.

---

* See Majorie Smith, "Where Credit is Due, " _Ms._, I: 36-37, October, 1972.

13

Banks, their Deposits (as of December 31, 1970) and their total employees (at year-end 1970). Note: employees in most cases are for the work force of the whole corporation, not just the bank itself.

BANK	DEPOSITS (in millions)	EMPLOYEES
Atlanta:		
Citizens & Southern	$ 1,378,858	3,550
First National Bank of Atlanta	789,464	2,335
Trust Company of Georgia	825,692	2,256
Chicago:		
Continental Illinois	7,154,425	8,207
First National Bank of Chicago	6,276,457	5,758
Northern Trust	1,741,447	2,424
Detroit:		
Detroit Bank & Trust	2,013,330	2,455
Manufacturers National Bank	1,913,478	2,491
National Bank of Detroit	4,000,462	5,822
New York:		
Chase Manhattan Bank	21,227,793	25,154
First National City Bank	21,085,459	37,000
Manufacturers Hanover	11,072,832	12,793
Philadelphia:		
First Pennsylvania Banking & Trust	2,517,626	6,525
Girard Bank	2,098,822	3,245
Philadelphia National Bank	2,038,932	3,070
Washington:		
American Security & Trust	695,437	1,208
National Bank of Washington	458,307	760
Riggs National Bank	884,279	2,041

Source: Moody's Bank & Finance Manual, 1971

Secondary Sources

During June and July 1971, secondary source material was examined. It included material published by banking industry trade associations; publications of the 18 sample banks; Federal rules and regulations relating to banks' employment and lending activities; and graduate studies from Harvard University and the University of Chicago. The files of the <u>American Banker</u> and <u>Bankers Magazine</u> were examined. The Leinsdorf (Nader-sponsored), Thieblot, and Corwin studies were read. Among the reference works consulted were: <u>Equal Employment Opportunity Report, Numbers One and Two: Job Patterns for Minorities and Women in Private Industry</u>, published by the Equal Employment Opportunity Commission in 1966 and 1967; <u>Hearings Before the U.S. Equal Employment Opportunity Commission on Discrimination in White Collar Employment</u>, January 15-18, 1968, published by E.E.O.C.; and <u>Equal Employment Opportunity: Compliance and Affirmative Action</u>, co-sponsored and published by tne National Association of Manufacturers and Plans for Progress, 1969.

Primary Sources

Primary sources included a C.E.P. questionnaire, E.E.O.C. forms and American Bankers Association surveys, and approximately 200 interviews conducted in person and by telephone.

A ten-page questionnaire was developed, covering (1) recruitment, hiring, training, and upgrading of minorities and women; and (2) loans in support of minority economic development. Criticism and comment on the questionnaire were sought from placement directors at major universities; heads of talent search agencies; senior executives at banks outside the sample; directors of minority economic development organizations; management consultants; and financial reporters.

Before the questionnaire was mailed, the Council's directors phoned each sample bank to present C.E.P.'s credentials, outline the nature of the study, and invite participation. The questionnaire was mailed in July, together with a cover letter and information about C.E.P. such as: news releases describing its previous studies; a list of its major subscribers; a copy of its bi-monthly journal, <u>Ecomomic Priorities Report</u>; and an interview during which its executive director and one of its board members underwent close questioning by a reporter for a management/ investor relations newsletter.

Approximately two weeks after the first mailing, C.E.P. phoned each bank again to offer to answer any questions about the Council or the study.

In late August, a second letter was sent to banks which were reluctant to cooperate. It requested their participation again and assured the banks that C.E.P. is an objective, unbiased research organization. It stated that the makeup of the sample would not be changed and that the names of banks declining to take part in the study would be published, together with whatever information about them could be obtained from other sources. In addition, the second mailing suggested that a bank which did not wish to complete the questionnaire might instead submit copies of two forms it had already filled out for other purposes--its latest Equal Employment Opportunity report (E.E.O.-1) and its most recent American Bankers Association urban affairs questionnaire.

Whenever a bank replied by supplying generalities or partial information, follow-up letters were sent expressing appreciation for the cooperation to date and renewing the request for specific information.

During October 1971-May 1972, from two to 18 hours of interviews were held each of 12 banks. They were conducted by the project directors and, on occasion, by the former management consultant. The banks themselves chose the interviewees: C.E.P. asked only that they be the people most responsible for minority employment, female employment, or minority lending. Some were compliance officers or vice presidents for personnel; others were executives in charge of minority economic development programs or urban affairs. The highest-ranking interviewee was an executive vice president, the lowest an assistant cashier; most often, respondents were vice presidents. At larger banks, up to five executives were interviewed.

Interviewers began by inviting questions about C.E.P., its purposes, and the sources of its funds. Respondents were then allowed to speak spontaneously, but they were asked standard questions within the relatively unstructured framework. In some instances, follow-up interviews were conducted by phone or in person. A number of lower-ranking bank employees were also interviewed, some with the knowledge and consent of management, others without; many were eager to comment on the practices of their respective institutions.

A variety of other interviews were conducted. Among the respondents were: representatives of community groups and minority rights organizations; feminists; representatives of banking industry trade associations; reporters from minority and majority newspapers; a taxi driver; a real estate agent; a guard at the Treasury Department in Washington; professors of business, law, and sociology; officials of the Treasury Department, Small Business Administration, Equal Employment Opportunity Commission, and the Federal Deposit Insurance Corporation; a city council member, a state legislator, a representative of a state human rights commission, and staff members of the U.S. House and Senate; authors of earlier studies of the banking industry; former employees of the 18 sample banks, and executives of minority-owned and white-owned banks outside the sample.

All data were checked for accuracy with cooperating banks in October and November of 1972.

Part 2

Cooperation and Resistance

Due to Federal restrictions, employment and lending data are virtually unobtainable unless a bank agrees to release them: the 1964 Civil Rights Act prohibits unauthorized disclosure of the former, and Small Business Administration policy prohibits unauthorized disclosure of the latter. Eleven of the 18 banks in the study either provided the Council on Economic Priorities with generalities in lieu of hard information or declined to provide any information at all. The president of one Detroit bank which would not cooperate reportedly accused C.E.P. of "attempting to undermine the free enterprise system."

This is the first in-depth Council study to meet resistance of this magnitude. Twenty-two of 24 companies cooperated with a study of pollution control in the pulp and paper industry titled Paper Profits.[1] A study of electric utilities and the environment, The Price of Power,[2] received cooperation from all of the 15 companies in the study.

Banks which declined to cooperate commonly cited two reasons: (1) that the requested information is classified as internal by bank policy, and is released only to government or "quasi-government" agencies; or (2) that a large number of similar requests have required excessive expenditures of time and money. In rebuttal, C.E.P. argued that the study did not duplicate any earlier research project; that little time or money would be required to provide the Council with copies of E.E.O.-1 forms and the American Bankers Association Urban Affairs Surveys, which the banks had already completed, as substitutes for C.E.P.'s own questionnaire; and that any other information requested was likely to be found on file, so that no special preparation was necessary.

Nonetheless, most banks responded that they were proud of their practices-- but did not want to make them public. Their annual reports often reflected the same attitude. They stressed the importance of corporate social responsibility but rarely indicated how much money was spent on social programs, how many people were involved, or how effective the programs were. The statements below, which were reminiscent of other industries' attempts to deal with social ills by means of public relations[3] were typical:

> Providing educational opportunities to help improve
> skills, develop managerial abilities, and prepare for
> promotion remains a prime concern of management. In
> this endeavor in-bank training programs continued at
> an accelerated pace and many staff members were enrolled
> in university courses and specialized business seminars.[4]

Within the last year, we have been involved in intensive efforts to provide jobs for the hard-core unemployed, in mortgage programs oriented toward the needs of the inner city area, and in new programs to help small businessmen, with particular emphasis on minority groups. We provided major assistance in helping to establish a new black-owned and managed bank in Detroit. and we are a vital part of a highly successful neighborhood improvement program. Project Pride, covering a 55-block area in Detroit's east side.[5]

The bank's responsibility to help improve the social and environmental aspects of the community represents a major concern of Philadelphia National Bank. It is our belief that the future success of the bank is closely tied to the well-being of the community P.N.B. serves.[6]

Only four of the 18 banks expressed an immediate willingness to supply statistics in response to the first letter of inquiry--Chase Manhattan, Citizens and Southern, First Pennsylvania, and Continental Illinois. Only one bank, First National of Chicago, responded to the alternate suggestion made in the second letter and provided an E.E.O.-1 form and an A.B.A. survey. These five institutions, together with Manufacturers Hanover and National Bank of Washington, ended by cooperating fully, providing statistical information and, with the exception of First of Chicago, permitting interviews with key staff members. They therefore formed the core of the study's data on individual banks. Two of these banks, Chase and Citizens & Southern, were rated "Very Good," in co-operation, the other five "Good." Six more banks provided partial information, refusing to supply statistics but agreeing to interviews, and were therefore rated "Fair"-- First National City, Girard, Manufacturers National of Detroit, National Bank of Detroit, Northern Trust, and Philadelphia National. Five banks declined all cooperation, for reasons detailed under "Bank Profiles," and were rated "Poor"--American Security and Trust, Detroit Bank and Trust, First National of Atlanta, Riggs National, and Trust Company of Georgia. Only banks whose cooperation was "Very Good" or "Good" provided sufficient information to permit C.E.P. to rate their performance. Eight of the 11 banks whose cooperation was "Poor" or "Fair" participated in a 1970 study of blacks in banking, for which they were assured of anonymity. Below, the banks are listed alphabetically with their cooperation ratings.

VERY GOOD	GOOD	FAIR	POOR
Chase	Continental Illinois	First National	American Security
Citizens &	First National Bank	City Bank	& Trust
Southern	of Chicago	Girard	Detroit Bank & Trus
	First Pennsylvania	Manufacturers	First National Bank
	Manufacturers	National	of Atlanta
	Hanover	National Bank	Riggs
	National Bank of	of Detroit	Trust Company of
	Washington	Northern Trust	Georgia
		Philadelphia	
		National Bank	

20

Notes

[1] Published by M.I.T. Press.

[2] To be published by M.I.T. Press.

[3] See "Corporate Advertising and the Environment," _Economic Priorities Report_, September-October 1971.

[4] Manufacturers National Bank of Detroit, _1970 Annual Report_, p.7.

[5] National Bank of Detroit, _1970 Annual Report_, p. 25.

[6] Philadelphia National Bank, _1970 Annual Report_, p.4.

Commercial Banking:
Jobs, Salaries, and Organization

Unlike other thrift institutions such as savings and loan associations and savings banks, only commercial banks offer checking (demand) accounts. They also supply savings accounts, loans, and trust department services to individuals and to the business sector and are therefore known as "full service banks."

Banks have historically served as training grounds for the entire financial community. Employees have received their basic experience at a bank, then left for greener--i.e. higher-salaried--pastures. The turnover rate for banking was about 20% in 1971; in better economic times, it has run as high as 40%. The industry therefore has a constant need for new talent, partly because most of its jobs are tedious and partly because its salaries are the lowest in the financial community.

A pyramidal employment structure is scarcely peculiar to the banking industry. Yet a sketch of jobs and salaries provides perspective for specific data about the number and distribution of minority and female employees at the banks in the C.E.P. sample.

A large urban bank may be organized into from four to 25 departments, or more. Departments usually include Lending, Trust, Personnel, and Operations, each headed by a senior or executive vice president who reports to top management. Many banks also have investment and loan committees which oversee policy and report to the president or chairman. Lending is divided into retail, commercial, and international sections. Trust department services include research and money management for trusts and pension funds. Personnel includes recruiting, hiring, and counseling. Operations, where checks and securities are processed, is the largest department of all and may contain 50% of the bank's total work force. For example, Chase Manhattan had 13 major departments as of February 1971, and 8,300 of the bank's 16,800 employees worked in Operations.[1] Together, Operations, Personnel, and similar support departments contain 60-70% of a bank's workers.

However, the majority of top executives are found not in Operations but in commercial and international departments, and, to a lesser degree, in trust departments. Commercial banks make money from four sources: interest and fees on loans; interest and dividends on investment securities; interest, profit, and commissions on trading accounts; and investment management fees. It follows, then, that the important jobs are located in these income-producing areas. Lending is the most vital area. A C.E.P. survey of 19 top executives at 13 of the sample banks reveals that 14 of these officials--all of whom are white men--attained their present status as chairman of the board, president, or chief operating officer by way of commercial or corporate lending. (Two more had held senior positions in trust departments; one had been an economist with the Federal Reserve; and the other two, both executives at Washington, D.C. banks, had held high political posts in the Federal government, one as a Cabinet member, the other as an ambassador.

The 18 sample banks employ 76,000 people. (Source: Equal Employment Opportunity Commission. Includes only those employees within standard metropolitan statistical areas. If workers employed by the banks' holding companies, subsidiaries, etc. are counted, the sample banks' work force totals 140,000, according to the Fortune 500 and Rand McNally's Bankers Blue Book.) Sixty-eight per cent of these employees hold office and clerical jobs. Such low-level, low-paid positions are also held by 70% of the workers in the entire industry. These jobs rarely require a college degree, and the duties they entail are often monotonous. By E.E.O.C. definition, these workers include secretaries, stenographers, typists, bookkeepers, cashiers, tellers, and messengers; they also include office-machine operators who sort and process checks and securities. According to the Bureau of Labor Statistics, average weekly salaries for proof-machine operators in 1969 (the last year for which data are available) ranged from $101.00 in New York to $79.50 in Philadelphia; tellers with over five years' experience earned from $142.00 to $109.00 per week in the same cities.[2] According to David Leinsdorf's report, entry-level jobs at First National City paid $84.62 a week; employees with limited typing ability started at $90.38 a week, while employees who were high school graduates with some business training began at $96.15. In contrast, college graduates recruited directly from the campus and assigned to an executive-management training program at Citibank received annual starting salaries of $201.92 per week and executive trainees who held M.B.A.s earned several thousand dollars more a year.[3]

Above office and clerical jobs are professional and technical positions, held by accountants, auditors, mathematicians, computer programmers, and others. Professionals customarily have a college degree or the equivalent; technical jobs call for about two years of post-high school education or the equivalent. These positions account for almost 10% of those in the C.E.P. sample at salaries ranging from $150 to $250 a week.[4]

Still higher up are jobs as officials and managers--middle- and upper-level positions held by loan officers, trust officers, department supervisors, and the like. Employees at the lower end of this category may earn as little as $7,000. But those at the upper end set policy and run the bank. They have the most interesting work, enjoy the greatest responsibility, and earn the most money--up to $200,000 a year. Officials and managers account for about 15% of the sample banks' work force. According to the Leinsdorf report, assistant cashiers earned from $10,400 to $33,500 at First National City; assistant vice presidents $18,750-$67,000; and senior vice presidents and executive vice presidents up to $100,000 a year.[5] The presidents and chairmen of three C.E.P. banks in New York all earned well over $100,000 in 1971, according to Business Week: Walter Wriston and William Spencer of First National City were paid $235,000 and $200,000; David Rockefeller and Herbert Patterson of Chase earned $230,000 and $172,000; and Gabriel Hauge and John

McGillicuddy of Manufacturers Hanover earned $200,000 and $135,000.[6] These earnings are, of cource, exclusive of fringe benefits, stock options, etc.

Notes

[1] Warren Conrad, second vice president, Chase Manhattan Bank, telephone interview, August 1972.

[2] Industry Wage Survey: Banking, November 1969 (Washington: U..S. Department of Labor, Bureau of Labor Statistics, 1971), pp.5-8.

[3] David Leinsdorf, project director, Citibank: A Preliminary Report by the Nader Task Force on First National City Bank (Washington: Center for the Study of Responsive Law, 1971), p.11.

[4] Industry Wage Survey, op. cit., pp.5-8.

[5] Leinsdorf, op. cit., p.11.

[6] Business Week, May 6, 1972.

Industry Associations

The three major industry-wide organizations in banking are the American Bankers Association, the National Bankers Association, and the National Association of Bank Women.

The American Bankers Association

The largest of these is the A.B.A. Its annual budget of $12 million is obtained through fees levied on member banks, which vary with the banks' size. It has a permanent staff of 300. Only two of the 100 professionals on that staff are members of minority groups; none of the senior clerical workers is non-white, but about 25% of the 75 clerical and support workers are. (The population of Washington, where the organization has its headquarters, is more than 70% black.)

During the last five years, the A.B.A. has consistently taken positions on behalf of increased minority employment and minority economic development activity by banks. As of August 1972, however, the organization has neither spoken for nor acted on the matter of female employment. Asked about the A.B.A.'s position on employment of women in banking, an organization representative replied, "We have no position."

A.B.A.'s efforts to stimulate minority employment and lending center in its Urban and Community Affairs Committee, whose president is Walter E. Hoadley, Jr., an executive vice president of the Bank of America. The committee has a professional staff of five. It has 40 members, six regional chairmen, and a four-member executive committee. Most of these 50 people are chairmen, vice chairmen, presidents, or executive vice presidents of major banks; in 13 cases, their banks rank among the nation's 50 largest. All are men, and only a smattering are non-white.

Day-to-day responsibility for the Urban and Community Affairs Committee rests with its director, Peter F. McNeish, a lawyer and former official of Pennsylvania's poverty program. Mr. McNeish says the Committee's role is necessarily limited to "suggestion and persuasion" because it exists primarily upon its members' sufferance.

To encourage minority employment and minority lending, the Committee's professional staff, plus black and white bankers who serve in A.B.A. workshops, travel around the country visiting member banks. The first page of one of the kits of literature they use in the process recognizes the element of self-interest, as well as that of social responsibility:

	Among the positive reasons...	Among the defensive reasons...	
POSITIVE AND DEFENSIVE REASONS	First, the economic growth of depressed areas is essential to the sound development of our urban areas and therefore to our banks. Banks are peculiarly tied to the urban areas in which they operate. Their corporate customers, however, are free to move if dissatisfied.	First, initiatives by the banking industry in urban problem-solving will help to forestall further encroachment of the private sector by governmental regulation.	Finally, banks should demonstrate a progressive corporate posture in attacking social problems.
WHY A BANK SHOULD PROMOTE			
MINORITY BUSINESS LENDING	Second, the medium-term outlook for increased profit potential of the minority market is quite attractive due to both the projected increase in minorities as a percentage of the population and also the projected rise in income levels of minority groups.	Second, there is considerable concern within the private sector that government-dictated solutions to urban problems might be: 1. more costly, resulting in increased taxes; 2. less efficient, resulting in compounding the problems; and 3. less effective, resulting in thwarted aspirations.	
	Third, banks as recipients of deposits from minority communities have an obligation to re-invest a fair share of those deposits back into the minority community.	Third, a sound economic structure should be created to ensure that the poverty areas will not expand to encompass other areas of the inner city where branches and customers are located.	
	Fourth, a strong minority-oriented program should enhance our efforts to attract executive talent from the leading colleges and business schools as well as clerical employees who are being drawn in increasing numbers from local minority communities.	Fourth, participation in an aggressive minority business lending program lessens the likelihood that personnel and property of the bank will be disturbed.	

Source: The American Bankers Association (Typed as printed)

The Urban and Community Affairs Committee is engaged in five programs:

A.B.A./National Urban League Fellowship Program: The Urban League's fellowship program began in 1965. In 1967-68, banking became one of the industries participating in it. The project is meant to give professors at black colleges an opportunity to gain practical business experience by spending their summers working in major corporations. It is hoped that the professors will later encourage students to seek careers in banking. According to Donald W. Woods, the Urban League official who oversees it, the program also gives host banks the opportunity to "strengthen their recruitment base." Applications for fellowships are processed by the Urban League, which then makes recommendations to the Urban Affairs Committee. Qualified candidates are referred to individual banks. While it is they who pay the fellows' expenses, not the A.B.A., the A.B.A. did finance the end-of-summer evaluation of the project by the fellows one year when the original Ford Foundation grant ran out. To date, the program has involved approximately 48 people and 27 banks, including two Federal Reserve Banks.

Six of the sample banks have participated in the project since 1968: First National City, Chase Manhattan, and Manufacturers Hanover have sponsored fellowships in each of the three years; Continental Illinois, First Pennsylvania, and Philadelphia National Bank have sponsored fellows in two years. A seventh bank, Citizens and Southern, offered to sponsor a professor last year, but all applicants were committed to other banks at the time of its offer.

Black Executive Exchange Program (B.E.E.P.): Like the A.B.A./Urban League Fellowship Program, B.E.E.P. is an attempt to increase contacts between white industry and black colleges. Unlike the fellowship program, it is not a joint A.B.A.-Urban League effort but an Urban League enterprise in which the A.B.A. takes part. In this case, black executives from white banks lecture students at black colleges in the area of their expertise. Expenses, including the lecturer's normal salary for the two days spent on campus, are borne by individual banks. A pilot B.E.E.P. project was run in 1968; the formal program began in 1970. The A.B.A.'s role has been to canvas member banks for qualified black executives.

Seven sample banks have participated in the Black Executive Exchange Program: First National City, Chase Manhattan, Manufacturers Hanover, Continental Illinois, National Bank of Detroit, First Pennsylvania, and Citizens and Southern.

Thomas I. Ahart of the Urban and Community Affairs Committee informed C.E.P. that the A.B.A. generally asks the top 300 U.S. banks to take part in both B.E.E.P. and the Urban League Fellowship Program. Since all sample banks are among the top 300, the following ten have presumably declined to participate in either one: American Security and Trust, Detroit Bank and Trust, First National of Atlanta, First National of Chicago, Girard, Manufacturers National of Detroit, National Bank of Washington, Northern Trust, Riggs, and Trust Company of Georgia. [1]

<u>Minbank Capital Corporation</u>: Minbank Capital Corporation is an invest-
ment firm owned and managed by the A.B.A. whose function is to supply
capital to minority banks. It was officially announced in July 1971.
Minbank has a projected capitalization of $10 million, to be raised
through sale of stock to A.B.A. member banks. Money obtained thereby
is in turn used to buy stock in minority banks. In most cases, the
stock is non-voting and therefore does not allow the A.B.A. to participate directly in management decisions.

To participate, a minority bank must have been in existence for more
than three years at the time Minbank began. Therefore, only 22 of the
34 banks which were then members of the National Bankers Association
qualified. Two sample banks, Chase Manhattan and National Bank of
Detroit, subscribed to the "maximum number of pre-incorporation
subscriptions offered them."[2]

<u>Key Cities Program</u>: Under this program, Urban and Community Affairs
Committee representatives visit high-ranking executives at banks in
major cities to urge that they act aggressively to increase minority
lending and minority hiring, instead of merely satisfying government
requirements. To facilitate this process, the A.B.A. encourages bankers
to form their own urban affairs committees. According to one A.B.A.
publication, 17 cities were visited in 1970 for the purpose of
stimulating black economic development, and such committees were set
up in 12 of them. The minority hiring aspect of the program began
in 1971; to date, six cities have been visited for that purpose.

<u>A.B.A./N.B.A. Management Training Program</u>: The status of this program,
discussed below, is in doubt. At the A.B.A.'s instigation, the two
organizations are now deciding whether to continue it and, if so, in
what form.

Surveys

Since 1970, the A.B.A. has attempted to monitor the activities of
member banks in the area of urban problems. To that end, the Urban
and Community Affairs Committee sends out an annual questionnaire
requesting information on minority employment, minority economic
development, and assistance to low- and middle-income housing. The
identities of banks which do--and do not--fill in the questionnaires
are not disclosed when the A.B.A. publishes the results.

The A.B.A.'s various programs affect only a small number of people,
and its preservation of banks' anonymity in the survey suggests public
relations rather than serious research.

The National Bankers Association

The National Bankers Association, the minority organization, was
founded in 1927 and has headquarters in Washington. It is considerably
smaller and less influential than the A.B.A. Its permanent staff
consists of six people, and its annual budget is $100,000, only 10%
of which was paid by its 36 member banks in 1970. The organization
has received a $200,000 grant from the Economic Development Administration.

Minority-owned and minority-managed banking is relatively fragile: the total assets of the minority banking community are $338,340,000--less than those of National Bank of Washington, the smallest bank in the C.E.P. sample. The N.B.A.'s largest member bank, Freedom National in New York, has deposits in excess of $45 million; the smallest, American State Bank in Tulsa, had assets of $1,516,101 as of December 31,1970.

The N.B.A. participated in a drive to increase minority banks' assets by obtaining $100 million in deposits by Fall 1971. Other participants were the A.B.A., the Treasury Department, and Capital Formation, a non-profit organization, funded mainly by the U.S. Office of Minority Business Enterprise, which provides management and technical aid to minority business. The $100 million goal was met, but critics complain that much of the money takes the form of highly volatile "tax and loan" accounts. The Federal government can, and does, call on banks to release these deposits on short notice, so that they cannot be used for long-term investments. On the other hand, calls are less likely to be made on smaller banks, and the monies have the advantage of being non-interest bearing accounts.

It has also been argued that minority banks cannot profitably invest what funds they do have for lack of skilled money managers. The dearth of management talent has been a prime concern of the N.B.A. As a result, the N.B.A. and A.B.A. have jointly run a management training program with the stated purpose of supplying personnel to minority banks. Trainees are sought and screened by both organizations, then given a stipend of $6,000-$9,000 and a year of intensive training at A.B.A. member banks. The first N.B.A./A.B.A. class had a total of 22 trainees, all males. Eleven of them were later placed in jobs at minority banks. The second class had a total of 37 trainees, including nine women. Only five of the 37 were placed.

Several reasons have been advanced for the program's failure to place trainees at minority banks. Graduates are under no legal obligation to accept such positions, and some have apparently taken jobs with white banks because they offer higher salaries. There is also some doubt about minority banks' ability and willingness to absorb graduates. One black banker in Philadelphia, who prefers to remain anonymous, suggests that the introduction of black management talent trained at white banks presents status problems for older, perhaps less well-trained executives. He claims that the N.B.A. did not anticipate this problem at the program's outset, and he therefore discounts the charge of another black banker that the program's covert purpose is to introduce black executives into white banks.

The National Association of Bank Women

No statement, and no action regarding female employment have come from the National Association of Bank Women. The Chicago-based organization, established in 1921, has a membership consisting of 8,000 female bank officers. Most of the members--3,159--hold the lowest-level job in the officer category, that of assistant cashier. Another 965 members are assistant vice presidents; 569 are full vice presidents; 18 are senior vice presidents; 30 are executive vice presidents; and 41 are presidents.

31

Only 86 are officers in operations departments, although the great majority of employees in operations are women everywhere in the industry. Only two members are real estate loan officers; two more are advertising managers. One is formally listed as a commercial loan officer.

Most N.A.B.W. members are middle-aged, conservative and white. An organization representative has said that the group would like to attract younger, perhaps more militant women, but that it must now reflect the views of the present membership. Many of the younger women officers interviewed by C.E.P. have chosen not to join it, and one called it "a big fat joke."

The N.A.B.W. has.concerned itself chiefly with providing graduate school scholarships to members and, in the words of one of its publications, with "attract[ing] young women into the banking field and encourag[ing] them to improve their technical and professional skills."[3] The organization has brought no legal challenges against banks which discriminate against women.

Notes

[1] Information on uncooperative banks provided by the National Urban League.

[2] Minbank Prospectus, p.4.

[3] National Association of Bank Women News, "A Brief Summary of Its History and Purpose(Chicago: National Association of Bank-Women,Inc, March 1971), p.2.

Employment: The Legal Context

Employment practices in the banking industry are affected by Federal civil rights legislation and by three Federal orders which are enforced primarily by the Department of the Treasury. Banking is also indirectly affected by court tests of discrimination occasioned by fair employment suits brought against corporations in other industries. And three suits now being brought against banks themselves may have a profound impact.

Legislation and Orders

Title VII of the Civil Rights Act of 1964 forbids employment discrimination on the basis of race, color, sex, religion, or national origin. It provides three methods of enforcement: (1) the Equal Employment Opportunity Commission, which the Act establishes, has the power to utilize "conferences, conciliation, and persuasion" to eliminate discrimination; (2) an aggrieved party who is dissatisfied with E.E.O.C.'s efforts may bring an action in the Federal courts; and (3) the Attorney General may bring suit in the government's name when a "pattern or practice" of discrimination is found.

The Equal Pay Act, which took effect in 1964, requires payment of equal salaries and wages for equal work. It is administered by the Wage-Hour Administration in the Department of Labor.

Executive Order 11246, issued in 1965, contains anti-discrimination provisions paralleling those in Title VII. In addition, it requires banks and other Federal contractors to take "affirmative action" to assure the attainment of equal employment objectives. An affirmative action plan is defined as a "set of specific and result-oriented procedures to which a [Federal] contractor commits himself to apply every good faith and effort,"[1] and it is required even when no court has ruled that an employer has discriminated. The order is administered by the Office of Federal Contract Compliance within the Department of Labor, which has, in turn, designated various agencies to carry out the bulk of the compliance work.

As a result of the Civil Rights Act and Order 11246, employers of more than 100 people and government contractors with 50 employees or more must file annual statistics on all their employees on a standard form, E.E.O.-1. The statistics must show: (1) sex; (2) race--i.e. Negro, Oriental, Spanish-surnamed American, or American Indian; and (3) level of employment according to specified occupational categories like officials and managers, professionals, technicians, sales workers, office and clerical workers, craftsmen, operatives, laborers, and service workers. By law, public access to E.E.O.-1 statistics is prohibited unless the contractor agrees to release them; they cannot be obtained by means of the Public Information Act.

Order 4, issued by the Department of Labor in 1970, requires that affirmative action plans be accompanied by written goals and timetables for the redress of employment inequities affecting racial and ethnic minorities.

Revised Order 4, issued in 1972, extends the provisions of the original order to women.

Enforcement: Treasury Department

Responsibility for obtaining banks' compliance with the three Federal orders rests with the Treasury Department's compliance section, formally called the Equal Opportunity Program. Like other compliance agencies, it is supposed to inspect 50% of its assigned contractors annually, and it has a wide variety of sanctions at its disposal: names of defaulting contractors may be published; the Justice Department may be notified; or proceedings may be instituted under Title VII. In addition, if a bank fails to comply, the Department can end its status as a Federal contractor, with the result that it can no longer be a repository for Federal funds, collect Federal taxes, or sell or cash bonds.

C.E.P. attempted to learn how Treasury determines whether a bank is in compliance, how it determines whether any existing deficiencies have been corrected, how information about a bank's record reaches members of the public, and how often Treasury has employed the sanctions available to it.

According to David Gottlieb, a program specialist in the compliance section, Treasury conducted compliance reviews at an estimated 350-400 banks during the past year, less than 3% of the nation's 14,000 commercial banks. (Another official of the same section, Inez Lee, put the number at 400 to 500.) Mr. Gottlieb states that the country's largest banks are the ones chosen for review. But he declined to release their names to C.E.P. on the grounds that the information is "not a matter of public record;" Treasury did not even review the world's largest bank, the Bank of America, until after a fair employment suit had been filed against it in U.S. District Court.[2]

Mr. Gottlieb says that the Department has found up to 17 deficiencies at a single bank. Asked by C.E.P. how Treasury determines whether an institution has corrected such deficiencies, he replied, "We generally take a bank at its word...They tell me they're doing X, Y, Z. How do I know they're telling me the truth?"

Bank employees are not necessarily aware of the results of a review. David Sawyer, director of the Equal Opportunity Program, told C.E.P. that "it's common knowledge that a bank doesn't have to tell its people whether it's in compliance." The Department does not maintain records on non-complying banks, either; in Mr. Gottlieb's words, "There just aren't that many." Nor has Treasury ever ended the contractor status of any major bank.

34

As a result of the Department's policies, C.E.P. could not find out whether the sample banks have been reviewed or whether those which have been reviewed are in compliance or not.

Enforcement: E.E.O.C.

A person who claims to be the victim of job discrimination by a bank may complain to the E.E.O.C. In response, E.E.O.C. may investigate, conciliate, and persuade, but it may not issue cease-and-desist orders and it is required to defer its intervention until a state's own fair employment commission, if any, has had the chance to act. While a new law, the Equal Employment Act of 1972, authorizes the agency to bring civil suit against an employer on the employee's behalf, the law's effect has yet to be felt.

The Commission's effectiveness is suggested by the fact that less than half the complaints filed with it through 1971 were successfully conciliated, even to a limited degree.[3] Last year, the U.S. Commission on Civil Rights assailed E.E.O.C. for failing to reduce its backlog of unresolved charges and denounced the "inertia [of] the Federal bureaucracy--in some cases a blind, unthinking fidelity to the status quo, in others a calculated determination to do nothing to advance the cause of civil rights."[4] One study has suggested that companies regulated by Order 11246 may actually have worse minority employment practices than other companies.[5]

Court Tests of Discrimination in Other Industries

Although the case law of employment discrimination is still at a relatively early stage of development, some of the ambiguities contained in Federal legislation have received substantial judicial interpretation.

In cases of overt bias, where discriminatory intent and effect are apparent, the only issue is one of proof. However, the courts have moved beyond this to hold that an employer's intent is irrelevant and that the key issue is whether company practices have unnecessarily discriminatory effects on groups protected by statute. (Griggs v. Duke Power Co., 401 U.S. 424. (1971). Gregory v. Litton Syst., 316 F. Supp. 401, 402 (C.O. Cal. 1970).

There is no universally accepted and legally defined statistical standard to prove that a firm is biased. But the introduction of statistical evidence to show disparity in the employment of whites and non-whites, or men and women, is essential in arguing a discrimination case.* Usually, the evidence presented is meant to show either (1) a disparity between the percentage of a group employed by a firm and that group's percentage of the local labor force or (2) a disparity between the percentage of a group employed by a firm and its percentage of a given job category.

---

* In the absence of statistical evidence regarding a differential impact on people protected by the Act, employers are not required to select workers on the basis of "merit" or to use job related tests.

The degree of disparity needed to prove the existence of bias has not been established. And the question of whether statistical evidence can be used to establish the existence of discrimination as a matter of law, or used only to establish a prima facie case, remains unresolved. In one court test Parham v. Southwestern Bell, 433, F. 2d 421 (8th Cir. 1970), the fact that 51 of a company's 2,736 employees were black was held to establish a violation of Title VII as a matter of law. In another, Brown v. Gaston City. Dining Machine Col, 457 F. 2d ·1377 (4th Cir. 1972) a court concluded that discrimination had occurred where less than 10% of a company's employees were blacks clustered in low-paying, low-status jobs, while the black population of the county was 13%.

Once the complainant has shown that employment standards exclude a disproportionate number of women or minority group members, the burden of proof of non-discrimination shifts to the employer. Practices which exclude blacks and which cannot be shown to be related to job performance are prohibited. (Griggs v. supra, at p. 431); the only standard which may be used to justify such practices is that of "business necessity." Practices which exclude women--or men--are allowable not only by that standard but in instances where sex is a "bona fide occupational qualification (bfoq)" reasonably necessary to the normal operation of a particular business; however, E.E.O.C. guidelines on sex as a "bfoq" stress that such exceptions should be narrowly construed. Individuals may not be refused employment because of assumptions or stereotypes about members of their sex as a class or because of the preference of employers, co-workers, clients, or customers.

Where bias has been found, courts have set precedents for the granting of affirmative relief. Extensive minority recruitment and hiring have been required, and victims of discrimination have been awarded back pay.

Court Tests of Discrimination in Banking

Several court tests directly affecting banks have been completed. In one suit, higher pay scales for male employees were held to be justified if greater effort, longer working hours, or other job responsibilities were involved. (Wirtz v. First Victoria National Bank) In another case, a bank policy which permitted only male employees to smoke was found to be discriminatory. (E.E.O.C. Decision No. 71-109, July 29, 1970) In a third instance, exclusion of women from a training program was ruled discriminatory and payment of lower wages to female tellers and bookkeepers than to males was ruled invalid. (Shultz v. First Victoria National Bank)

Finally, several major court cases alleging sexist practices in the banking industry are now underway in Texas, New York, and California. For a discussion of the Weal, Wadsworth, and Bank of America suits, see "Women: Legal Challenges," page 70.

Notes

[1] David Sawyer, "Guidelines-Affirmative Action Programs for Banks, Savings and Loan Associations, and Savings Banks" (Washington: Office of the Secretary of the Treasury, no date), p.1.

[2] Barbara Phillips, attorney for the plaintiffs, telephone interview, August 1972.

[3] "Developments in the Law: Employment Discrimination and Title VII of the Civil Rights Act of 1964," 84 Harvard Law Review, 1971, pp. 1109, 1201, 1316.

[4] The Federal Civil Rights Enforcement Effort: One Year Later (no place: U.S. Civil Rights Commission, Clearinghouse publication no. 34, November 1971), p.vi.

[5] "Executive Order 11246 Anti-Discrimination Obligation in Government Contracts," 44 New York University Law Review, 1969, p. 590.

Employment: The Status Quo

Introduction

According to Equal Employment Opportunity Commission aggregate data for 1970, the 18 sample banks--which are the three largest in each of six cities--employ a total of 76,000 workers. As explained in "Commercial Banking: Jobs, Salaries, and Organization," these people work in four main categories: blue collar and service; office and clerical; professional, technical, and sales; and official and managerial.

C.E.P. analyzed employment statistics from the sample banks, looking at each type of job and what sort of employees hold it. Then C.E.P. ascertained the probability that an employee of a given race and sex will be assigned to a given job category. Both methods were applied to three-bank aggregate data and to data for those individual banks which provided enough information for the purpose. The composition of each bank's entire work force and the composition of each city's labor force were also examined.

Seven banks supplied employment data to C.E.P. Six of them released copies of their 1971 E.E.O.-1 forms, thereby enabling the Council to analyze the information by race and sex; the seventh bank, Continental Illinois, combined its data for white and minority women and for male and female minorities, so that only a partial analysis was possible.

The cross-checking and comparisons reveal that clear employment patterns do exist and that they hold true both for individual banks and for aggregate data. In most cities, E.E.O.C. three-bank aggregate data does not cover all branches within the metropolitan area, only the largest branches within the city proper; therefore, employees at other branches do not appear in the Commission's statistics. For example, E.E.O.C. data for the three largest banks in Atlanta include only five units; Citizens and Southern reported to the Commission that it has one minority female in the official-managerial category, yet that employee is not listed in E.E.O.C. aggregate information. At C.E.P.'s insistence, E.E.O.C. rechecked its aggregate data several times.

The patterns are summarized on the next two tables. The first shows the composition of each job category, by race and sex, at all sample banks. The second shows the probability that a person of a given race and sex, once hired, will be found in a particular job category.

DISTRIBUTION OF JOBS
18 Sample Banks

Categories as a Percentage of all Jobs		Percentage Held by Race and Sex			
		White		Minority	
Categories	%	M	F	M	F
Officials and Managerial	17.4%	81.3%	12.8%	3.8%	2.2%
Professional, Technical, & Sales	9.8	69.2	21.7	6.4	2.7
Office & Clerical	68.7	19.0	48.3	8.3	24.5
Blue Collar & Service	4.1	54.1	13.9	25.5	6.4

PROBABILITY OF EMPLOYMENT IN VARIOUS CATEGORIES
BY RACE AND SEX*
18 Sample Banks

OFFICIALS AND MANAGERS

White Males	Minority Males	White Females	Minority Females
1/3	1/12	1/17	1/48

PROFESSIONALS, TECHNICIANS & SALESWORKERS

White Males	Minority Males	White Females	Minority Females
1/5	1/13	1/18	1/67

OFFICE AND CLERICAL

Minority Females	White Females	Minority Males	White Males
1/1	1/1	1/1	1/3

BLUE COLLAR AND SERVICE WORKERS

Minority Males	White Males	White Females	Minority Females
1/8	1/16	1/67	1/77

* Listed in ascending order by the small percentage differences which exist.
To obtain these probabilities, which are based upon E.E.O.C. data for the 18 sample banks, C.E.P. divided the percentage of a particular group of workers located in a particular job category into 1.0, then rounded off to the nearest whole number. For example, 2.05% of the black women employed by sample banks are officials and managers, and .0205 divided into 1.0 equals 48; therefore, the probability that a worker of that race and sex will be found in that job category is one in 48.

Three-Bank Aggregates

In each of the six cities studied, women are employed at a level exceeding their representation in the local labor force, with the most notable difference occuring in Detroit.

WOMEN AS A PERCENTAGE OF CITY LABOR FORCE
AND AS A PERCENTAGE OF ALL BANK EMPLOYEES
Three-Bank Aggregates

CITY	% LABOR FORCE*	% TOTAL BANK	DIFFERENCE (Percentage Points)
Atlanta	45.3%	57.3%	+ 12.0
Chicago	41.3	50.9	+ 9.6
Detroit	38.7	65.2	+ 26.5
New York	40.7	54.7	+ 14.0
Philadelphia	41.2	57.8	+ 16.6
Washington	48.8	58.9	+ 10.1

Minority group members, however, are employed at levels below their share of the city labor force in all cities except New York, with the difference most conspicuous in Washington and Atlanta.

MINORITIES AS A PERCENTAGE OF CITY LABOR FORCE
AND AS A PERCENTAGE OF ALL BANK EMPLOYEES
Three-Bank Aggregates

CITY	% LABOR FORCE*	% TOTAL BANK	DIFFERENCE (Percentage Points)
Atlanta	50.2%	13.9%	- 36.3
Chicago	33.4	18.2	- 15.2
Detroit	42.2	18.9	- 23.3
New York	25.6	31.8	+ 6.2
Philadelphia	32.1	17.0	- 15.1
Washington	70.4	33.4	- 37.0

Individual Banks

Women constitute more than half the employees at six of the seven reporting banks, and nearly half the staff at the remaining institution. They are therefore more heavily represented in each bank's work force than in each city's labor force.

* Source: Bureau of the Census. Percentages include Negroes and Spanish-Surnamed Americans, but not American Indians or Orientals.

41

WOMEN AS A PERCENTAGE OF CITY LABOR FORCE
AND AS A PERCENTAGE OF ALL EMPLOYEES
Seven Reporting Banks

BANK	% LABOR FORCE	% BANK POPULATION	DIFFERENCE (Percentage Points)
(Atlanta)			
Citizens & Southern	40.7%	60.8%	+ 20.1
(Chicago)			
Continental Illinois	41.3	52.5	+ 11.2
First National Bank	41.3	48.3	+ 7.0
(New York)			
Chase Manhattan	40.7	54.5	+ 13.8
Manufacturers Hanover	40.7	55.7	+ 15.0
(Philadelphia)			
First Pennsylvania	41.2	59.6	+ 18.4
(Washington)			
National Bank	48.8	57.3	+ 8.5

Minorities are under-represented compared with the city labor force at
all banks outside New York, with differences ranging from 12 points at
the two Chicago banks reporting to 36 points at National of Washington.
Minority representation in the bank population is slightly above the
labor force level only at the two New York banks responding.

MINORITIES AS A PERCENTAGE OF CITY LABOR FORCE
AND AS A PERCENTAGE OF ALL EMPLOYEES
Seven Reporting Banks

BANK	% LABOR FORCE	% BANK POPULATION	DIFFERENCE (Percentage Points)
(Atlanta)			
Citizens & Southern	50.2%	17.3%	- 32.9
(Chicago)			
Continental Illinois	33.4	20.3	- 13.1
First National Bank	33.4	21.2	- 12.2
(New York)			
Chase Manhattan	25.6	30.2	+ 4.6
Manufacturers Hanover	25.6	28.9	+ 3.3
(Philadelphia)			
First Pennsylvania	32.1	13.4	- 18.7
(Washington)			
National Bank	70.4	24.3	- 36.1

Blue Collar and Service Worker Jobs

Three-Bank Aggregates

Blue collar and service positions constitute about 5% of all jobs at the banks.* More than 75% of them are held by men: about half the workers in the category are white males, and another quarter are minority males. In two cities, the concentration of minority group members in the category is massive: in Washington nearly 90% of all janitors, maids, attendants, etc. are minority men and women, and in Atlanta the figure is almost 83%. The percentage of these jobs held by white women is highest in Chicago; that for minority females is highest in Atlanta and Washington. In all other sample cities the least desirable, dead-end jobs do not seem to be restricted to minorities or women.

| | PERCENTAGE OF JOBS HELD BY | | | |
| | WHITE | | MINORITY | |
CITY	M	F	M	F
Atlanta	15.1%	2.1%	40.1%	42.7%
Chicago	52.6	33.8	10.7	2.9
Detroit	51.5	10.6	35.9	1.9
New York	72.6	4.6	20.7	2.1
Philadelphia	46.8	17.1	30.5	5.7
Washington	9.1	1.1	66.8	23.0

Individual Banks

A similar pattern emerges at the individual banks reporting. Blue collar-service jobs account for less than 10% of all jobs at each bank. The great majority of such positions are held by men, with percentages running from 73% at Citizens and Southern to 100% at First of Chicago. At two of the banks, lafge numbers of these jobs are filled by minority group members: at Citizens and Southern, nearly half the blue collar and service workers are minority people, and at National of Washington the concentration is 91%.

---

* Figures in the text of this chapter are rounded off to the nearest integer, those in the tables to the nearest tenth of one per cent.)

CITY	PERCENTAGE OF JOBS HELD BY			
	WHITE		MINORITY	
	M	F	M	F
(Atlanta)				
Citizens & Southern	49.7%	2.7%	23.5%	24.2%
(Chicago)				
Continental Illinois	----------data refused----------			
First National Bank	90.8	0.5	9.2	0.0
(New York)				
Chase Manhattan	64.6	6.7	26.4	2.4
Manufacturers Hanover	67.5	5.5	26.4	0.6
(Philadelphia)				
First Pennsylvania	64.7	2.4	29.3	3.6
(Washington)				
National Bank	9.3	0.0	76.0	14.7

Office and Clerical Jobs

Three-Bank Aggregates

Just above the blue collar and service level is office and clerical work. Approximately 70% of all employees in the sample perform office and clerical work and more than two-thirds of them are women, with percentages as high as 87% in Detroit. Slightly less than half the clerical workers are white females, and another 25% are minority females. The percentage of white men in this type of job is less than 28% in every city studied.

CITY	PERCENTAGE OF JOBS HELD BY			
	WHITE		MINORITY	
	M	F	M	F
Atlanta	20.9%	64.1%	3.7%	11.3%
Chicago	27.2	48.7	5.9	18.2
Detroit	10.1	67.4	2.4	20.1
New York	17.8	40.7	11.5	30.0
Philadelphia	21.3	60.1	3.7	14.9
Washington	16.3	47.2	9.4	27.1

Individual Banks

A parallel situation exists at the reporting banks where office and clerical employees comprise about two-thirds of all jobs at each of the banks. As in the aggregates, women account for a large majority of all of these employees, comprising from 68% at First National of Chicago to 77% of them at First Pennsylvania.

	PERCENTAGE OF JOBS HELD BY			
	WHITE		MINORITY	
CITY	M	F	M	F
(Atlanta)				
Citizens & Southern	24.8%	57.5%	4.3%	13.4%
(Chicago)				
Continental Illinois	----------data refused-------------			
First National Bank	25.5	45.2	6.2	23.1
(New York)				
Chase Manhattan	19.3	42.7	11.4	26.6
Manufacturers Hanover	18.7	44.1	9.7	27.5
(Philadelphia)				
First Pennsylvania	20.2	65.2	3.4	11.4
(Washington)				
National Bank	18.8	61.0	8.6	11.6

Professional, Technician, and Sales Jobs

Three-Bank Aggregates

Professional, technician,and sales jobs account for almost 10% of
those in the sample.* About 70% are held by white men and another
20% by white women. In five cities, however, minority men are employed
in the category at levels which are commensurate with their share of
the bank staff. (That share is, as stated, well below minorities'
share of the city labor force.)

Atlanta is an exception on two counts. There, a comparatively large
percentage of professional, technical, and sales jobs--almost 40%-- are
held by women. And although minorities account for more than 52% of the
city labor force, they constitute only about 1% of all workers in the
category.

	PERCENTAGE OF JOBS HELD BY			
	WHITE		MINORITY	
CITY	M	F	M	F
Atlanta	60.1%	38.4%	0.9%	0.5%
Chicago	76.2	16.5	6.0	1.3
Detroit	77.3	14.5	5.6	2.6
New York	65.4	24.2	6.7	3.7
Philadelphia	74.7	15.6	9.5	0.2
Washington	67.9	17.9	10.7	3.6

---

* The three types of jobs are usually grouped, but few banking industry
positions come under the heading of sales work.

Individual Banks

At individual reporting banks, again, the great majority of professionals, technicians, and sales workers are white men. First Pennsylvania has the highest percentage--83%--Manufacturers Hanover the lowest--60%. The share of these jobs assigned to white women never exceeds 23%, and the maximum percentages held by minority men and minority women are 15% and 4%, respectively.

| | PERCENTAGE OF JOBS HELD BY | | | |
| | WHITE | | MINORITY | |
CITY	M	F	M	F
(Atlanta)				
Citizens & Southern	65.0%	22.5%	8.8%	3.8%
(Chicago)				
Continental Illinois	------------data refused-----------			
First National Bank	67.6	19.5	10.5	2.4
(New York)				
Chase Manhattan	66.3	21.3	9.2	3.2
Manufacturers Hanover	60.1	22.1	15.1	2.6
(Philadelphia)				
First Pennsylvania	82.8	10.6	6.3	0.3
(Washington)				
National Bank	---------no jobs in category---------			

Official and Managerial Jobs

Three-Bank Aggregates

Official and managerial jobs, which stand at the top of the hierarchy, are more consistently white and male than any other type. While only 36% of all employees at the 18 banks are white males, 81% of all officials and managers are white men. Philadelphia has the highest representation with 94% and Washington the lowest with 78%.

In contrast, only 13% of all officials and managers are white women; an additional 4% are minority men; and another 2% are minority women. These three percentages are far below those groups' representation in the city labor force and bank population. White women fare worst in Philadelphia, where they hold only 3% of the upper-echelon jobs. Minorities fare worst in Atlanta, where E.E.O.C. aggregate data show that minority men (Hispanic Americans, in this instance) comprise one half of one per cent of the executives at the three banks and that none of the executives are minority women.

	PERCENTAGE OF JOBS HELD BY			
	WHITE		MINORITY	
CITY	M	F	M	F
Atlanta	86.6%	12.9%	0.5%	0.0%
Chicago	86.1	11.1	2.3	0.5
Detroit	79.1	16.2	2.3	2.4
New York	78.6	13.2	5.1	3.1
Philadelphia	94.4	3.4	1.6	0.6
Washington	78.4	16.0	3.9	1.7

Individual Banks

Similarly, the top jobs at the individual banks are customarily assigned to white males. The percentages of official and managerial positions held by white men is as high as 90% at First Pennsylvania and is no lower than 71% at Manufacturers Hanover. Most of the remaining employees in the category are white women, with the highest percentage--22%--at Manufacturers Hanover and the lowest--6%--at First Pennsylvania. Neither minority males nor minority females account for as much as 5% of all officials and managers at any bank.

	PERCENTAGE OF JOBS HELD BY			
	WHITE		MINORITY	
CITY	M	F	M	F
(Atlanta)				
Citizens & Southern	83.1%	15.5%	1.0%	0.3%
(Chicago)				
Continental Illinois	------------data refused----------			
First National Bank	84.6	11.7	2.9	0.7
(New York)				
Chase Manhattan	80.6	12.6	4.8	2.1
Manufacturers Hanover	71.0	21.9	4.2	2.9
(Philadelphia)				
First Pennsylvania	90.2	5.8	3.8	0.2
(Washington)				
National Bank	87.4	10.1	2.5	0.0

Probabilities: Officials and Managers

Three-Bank Aggregates

In every city studied, white men have the best chance of obtaining executive level positions--either one chance in two or one in three. Minority females have the poorest chance to reach that upper level of any group of employees--from zero in Atlanta to 1/35 and 1/38 in Detroit and New York, where their opportunities are greatest.

Minority males and white females fall between the other two groups of workers. The likelihood that a minority male will become an official or manager ranges from 1/11 in Detroit and New York to 1/43 in Atlanta. The probability for white females ranges from 1/14 in New York and Washington to 1/111 in Philadelphia.

PROBABILITY OF EMPLOYMENT AS OFFICIALS AND MANAGERS

CITY	WHITE		MINORITY	
	M	F	M	F
Atlanta	1/2	1/19	1/43	Zero
Chicago	1/3	1/21	1/15	1/143
Detroit	1/2	1/18	1/11	1/34
New York	1/2	1/14	1/11	1/38
Philadelphia	1/3	1/111	1/27	1/166
Washington	1/2	1/14	1/19	1/71

Individual Banks

Roughly the same picture appears at the individual reporting banks. White men have the best chance of obtaining an official or managerial job--from 1/2 at National of Washington and Manufacturers Hanover to 1/4 at Citizens and Southern. Likewise, minority females have the poorest chance--a minimum of zero at National of Washington to a maximum of 1/29 at Manufacturers Hanover.

At Manufacturers Hanover, white females have the best chance to reach the upper echelon: at that institution, the figure is 1/7 as against 1/2 for white males. In contrast, the probability that a white woman will become an official or manager at First Pennsylvania is only 1/62.

Minority men have the greatest chance to attain the official-managerial level at First Pennsylvania and the least at Citizens and Southern--1/9 and 1/44, respectively.

PROBABILITY OF EMPLOYMENT AS OFFICIALS AND MANAGERS

BANK	WHITE		MINORITY	
	M	F	M	F
(Atlanta)				
Citizens & Southern	1/4	1/43	1/27	1/333
(Chicago)				
Continental Illinois	--------Data Refused		----------	
First National Bank	1/3	1/11	1/14	1/100
(New York)				
Chase Manhattan	1/3	1/15	1/19	1/67
Manufacturers Hanover	1/2	1/10	1/7	1/29
(Philadelphia)				
First Pennsylvania	1/3	1/9	1/63	1/333
(Washington)				
National Bank	1/2	1/37	1/30	Zero

48

Distribution of Minority and Female Executives

In the main, the distribution of minority and female executives does not afford them maximum opportunities for prestige, high salaries, and advancement to the top-most rungs.

The primary source of a bank's income is interest and fees earned on loans, and the largest share of loan income derives from commercial lending. As an illustration, First Pennsylvania's 1971 annual report states that the bank and its subsidiaries earned $200,900,000 from loans, 80.2% of which came from commercial lending, 11.7% from consumer (i.e. retail) lending, and 8.1% from mortgage and real estate lending.

It is not surprising, then, that most presidents, chairmen, and chief operating officers at C.E.P. banks attained their present status by way of commercial lending. (See "Commercial Banking: Jobs, Salaries, and Organization.") Yet the area has historically been closed to minorities and women. Today, it remains very male and very white. C.E.P. staff members observed four commercial lending departments--two in Detroit and two more in Chicago. Few minority males were seen, and every woman observed had a typewriter at her desk. Only one of the 8,000 members of the National Association of Bank Women is formally listed as a commercial lending officer.

Female officials and managers seldom have charge of operations departments, either, although the vast majority of employees in those departments are women and many are minority women; only 86 N.A.B.W. members are listed as operations officers.[1] Instead, female executives are most often found in personnel departments or in branch banking, where the lending activity is retail-oriented and the size of the loans comparatively small.

Other Job Categories

Where office and clerical work is concerned, the probability that a white or minority group woman will be relegated to such a position is always 1/1, both in three-bank aggregate data and at individual reporting banks. The likelihood for men of all races is 1/1 to 1/4 at the aggregates and 1/1 to 1/3 at the reporting banks.

White and minority men are most likely, and women least likely, to be found working in a blue collar-service worker capacity. Atlanta is an exception among cities: there, minority women have a far greater chance than white males to hold jobs in this category. Similarly, minority women are more likely than white men to be blue collar or service workers at Citizens and Southern and National of Washington than at other institutions reporting.

Probability tables for professional-technical-sales, office-clerical, and blue collar-service jobs appear in Appendix IV, page 166.

In short, any male employee, once hired, is more likely than any female employee to be an official or manager or a blue collar or service worker. However, any man is less likely than any woman to hold an office-clerical job.

Summary

In broad terms, the following statistical patterns emerge from the aggregate data:

1.) Blue collar and service worker jobs tend to be filled by men (75%), and at Washinton and Atlanta banks by minority group members.

2.) Office and clerical jobs are overwhelmingly filled by women (70%).

3.) Professional, technician and sales workers jobs tend to be held by white men (70%). Few women of any race perform these jobs.

4.) The official-managerial category, at the top of the bank hierarchy, is almost entirely filled by white men (80%); few white women, fewer minority men, and still fewer minority women are officials and managers. Because the individuals holding these jobs control lending practices and a wide variety of policies, this is perhaps the most significant fact of all.

Substantially the same patterns hold true for individual banks reporting, with the exception of Manufacturers Hanover, which has a somewhat larger percentage of women in official and managerial positions (25%).

Notes

1
    "NABW List of Titles," National Association of Bank-Women, Inc., March 1971.

50

Changing the Status Quo

Four indices of any bank's effort to change the current employment mix are: recruitment; ratings; executive-management training programs; and promotions to officer. Data in all four areas suggest that minorities and women will not attain positions of power and authority in the near future.

Recruitment

Neither black talent search agencies nor placement directors on predominately black campuses--where more than a third of the country's black college students are enrolled--are convinced that banks are serious about recruiting minorities. C.E.P.'s inquiries consistently revealed anxiety and distrust of bankers' motives.

The placement director of Howard University, Sam Hall, says that many corporate recruiters leave the campus without hiring anyone because they seek blacks who can "walk water" and that some black recruiters, themselves Howard alumni, are "super blacks" looking for more "super blacks." Another director says that "corporations recruit here because they have to. The government is down on them." An executive of a major black talent search agency headquartered in New York, Richard Clark Associates, says that "most corporations are looking for a black guy who is white." "Back in the early 1960's," he adds, "they wanted a light-skinned Negro with curly hair; now they want to hire people who look black but act white." The head of a Detroit agency maintains that he sees more qualified people than banks are willing to hire, and one agency staff member says that "they just don't seem to be concerned."

At the same time, bank recruiters are less than enthusiastic about minority employment agencies. Several say that the agencies charge too much for their services and "could not go any place the bank itself could not go." Banks also complain about the level of "no-shows" on minority campuses--students who sign up for appointments then fail to appear. One personnel officer says he repeatedly telephoned the placement director of a black college in the south to confirm that a number of interviews had been scheduled, but found neither students nor placement director on hand when he arrived. A personnel officer at a large Philadelphia bank recounts a similar incident at a predominately black university in Pennsylvania. As a result of the incident, the bank has not recruited on that campus for four years.

Several placement directors at black schools vigorously deny the existence of a no-show problem. Sam Hall maintains that "black colleges have no more of a no-show problem than any of the white schools."

W. Kirk Jackson of Atlanta University says he has a strict rule on the subject: "The only excuse for a student who fails to show for an appointment is a death in the family. His own."

Placement directors and bank executives do agree that the competition for minority holders of M.B.A.'s is so intense that these students receive salary offers up to $2,000 higher than those made to their white counterparts. Asked about this, a senior bank official in Detroit says, "We just can't compete on that level." But the president of a minority bank in Minneapolis replies, "Yeah, but it's catch-up allowance."

Less effort is made to recruit women on campus than blacks. Most sample banks which visit predominantly female schools began doing so very recently. First National City did no such recruitment until this year. Manufacturers Hanover was scheduled to go to Connecticut College but cancelled without explanation. Chase recruited at Barnard. First Pennsylvania went to a women's college for the first time in 1972, interviewing ten students at Beaver College in Pennsylvania but making no job offers. According to an official of Beaver, no other bank appeared there at all.

Senior vice president Walter Powell holds First Pennsylvania's own staff responsible for the poor record. But other banks have harsh words for college placement officials. A female recruiter at Citibank says that placement bureaus at women's schools are usually useful only at the graduate level. Some banks complain that bureaus either tell female students that banks "won't hire you" or neglect to inform them that bank representatives are coming to the campus to meet them.

Eleven sample banks say they recruit on black campuses; five more provided no response. Seven banks say they recruit at women's campuses: Manufacturers Hanover, Chase, First National City, First Pennsylvania, Citizens and Southern, First of Chicago, and Continental Illinois; three others say they do not: Girard, National Bank of Detroit, and Detroit Bank and Trust; seven declined to reply. The eighteenth bank, National of Washington, does no college recruiting because of its small size.

RECRUITING AT PREDOMINANTLY BLACK & FEMALE COLLEGES
1970

| | Black | | White | | |
	Number Colleges Visited	Number of Hires	Number Colleges Visited	Number of Hires	Total Colleges Visited
Chase Manhattan	11	25*	no ans.	138**	73
Citizens & Southern	12	9	1	6	44
Continental Illinois	9	0	3	75**	70
F.N.B., Chicago	no ans.	10*	no ans.	11*	no ans.
First Pennsylvania	5	0	0	0	26
Manufactuers Hanover	3	0	0	0	24
National of Washington			no college recruiting		

* Includes all hires of women and minorities with college degrees.
**Includes recruitment at coed schools.

Rating Systems

All sample banks for which information is available use some form of performance appraisal or rating system for evaluating employees' past work and future potential. Because promotions and salary increases may depend upon them, ratings become a significant factor in the upward mobility of minorities and women. First Pennsylvania, Continental Illinois, and Manufacturers Hanover confirmed that their employees must be rated before they can receive promotions or raises.

Usually, an employee's immediate supervisor analyzes and comments on her or his progress and on any problems that may have arisen. Banks often attempt to compensate for the inherently subjective nature of the procedure by soliciting comments from all concerned parties-- the supervisor, the department head, and, most important, the employee.

Thirteen of the 18 banks supplied information on their ratings. All state that supervisors are supposed to discuss them with employees. At nine of the 13, the employee is also supposed to see and sign or initial the report: Chase, Manufacturers Hanover, First National City, Continental Illinois, First National of Chicago, Northern Trust, Manufacturers National, National of Washington, and Citizens and Southern. Although First National of Atlanta did not release any data, one of its female officers stated that the same practice is followed there. Four more banks indicated that ratings need merely be discussed with the employee, not signed: National of Detroit, Girard, Philadelphia National, and First Pennsylvania.

Conducting appraisals is a time-consuming task, and follow-up utilization of them is rare. Some banks, notably Chase and Citizens and Southern, are exploring possible use of computers to indicate basic job skills, career paths, and the like. A related system is already in effect at Manufacturers Hanover.

The possibilities for discriminatory use of ratings are obvious. One woman at a large New York bank commented that appraisals are "like putting the cart before the horse." Regardless of how they are supposed to work, she continued, the consensus is that they merely reinforce a supervisor's previous inclination--or reluctance--to grant a promotion or raise.

The Council on Economic Priorities asked Walter Powell, senior vice president for personnel at First Pennsylvania, about possible bias. Mr. Powell denied that it occurs but admitted that he could not offer any foolproof method for insuring fair treatment. Mr. Powell indicated that his bank encourages supervisors to show reports to workers and to solicit their signatures. But he said that First Pennsylvania will not make this practice official policy until 1974 because the bank does not trust its supervisors' objectivity and wants to sensitize them to the problems of minorities and women before the policy change takes effect.

Some of the employment discrimination suits currently being brought against banks allege that performance appraisals are used with sexist intent. Beverly Wadsworth told C.E.P. that First National City asked her to initial a partially blank report of her work and used ratings in attempts to transfer her out of the commercial lending department. Another former employee of First National City, a woman who worked on the staff of the bank's training programs, commented that she had never been shown her ratings during her four years of employment.

In contrast, several other Citibank employees, including one minority male, have stated that the bank does indeed adhere to its policy of permitting employees to see and initial their reports.

Thus, the concept behind ratings is an equitable one, but opportunities for irregularities in their application are readily apparent.

Executive-Management Training Programs

Banking seldom recruits executives from outside. It promotes from within. Consequently, a bank's top officials come largely from its own management training programs. Robert Feagles, senior vice president for personnel at First National City, told C.E.P. that Citibank's college training program will "...hopefully supply, in the long run, the senior decision-makers of the organization." Another bank, Chase Manhattan, calls its credit training program its "principal source of officers."[1]

The content, duration, and structure of these training programs differ from bank to bank. They are variously named credit training, college training, or credit workshops. All of them combine on-the-job learning with formal, in-house course instruction, and all of them train people to be officers. It is here that an employee on the way up obtains the credentials needed for commercial lending. Most trainees are newly-graduated from colleges and universities. For example, 17 of the 20 trainees in First Pennsylvania's credit workshops so far this year were recruited from the campus.

---

[1] Chase Manhattan Corp., 1971 Annual Report, p.29.

Minority and female participation in executive-management training programs at sample banks is minimal. C.E.P. obtained data on 2,669 participants for the years 1968-70; only 233 or 8.7% of them were women, and only 188 or 7.0% were minority males or minority females. Of the 1,003 participants at six banks during 1970, only 100 trainees or 10% were women; all but 11 of the women were white; there were 72 minority males or 7.2% of the total.

As the table below indicates, during 1970 Continental Illinois ranked best in regard to females, with 18.9% of its trainees women; Citizens & Southern ranked worst with 4.4%. In regard to minorities, National Bank of Washington had the highest percentage, 25%, and Citizens and Southern the lowest, 3.7%. But "highest percentage" meant little at National of Washington because only 12 trainees of all races and both sexes took part in the program, so that "25%" amounted to only three minority men.

MINORITIES AND WOMEN AS A PERCENTAGE OF PARTICIPANTS IN EXECUTIVE-MANAGEMENT TRAINING PROGRAMS, 1970

	White Females	Minority Females	Minority Males	Total Females	Total Minorities
Continental Illinois	16.9	2.0	5.5	18.9	7.5
First Pennsylvania	8.9	2.2	11.1	11.1	13.3
Manufacturers Hanover	7.9	1.7	11.3	9.6	13.0
Chase Manhattan	8.0	0.6	5.2	8.6	5.7
National of Washington	8.3	0.0	25.0	8.3	25.0
Citizens and Southern	4.4	0.0	3.7	4.4	3.7

Only three banks--Continental Illinois, First Pennsylvania, and National Bank of Washington--had a larger proportion of women trainees than women executives. For minority males, the picture was even more discouraging; only at National Bank of Washington were they represented more heavily as executive trainees than as current holders of jobs above the office and clerical level.

First-Time Promotions to Officer

Recent promotions to the officer level--i.e. assistant cashier, assistant treasurer, or above--have not changed employment patterns.

Six banks supplied data on upgrading of this kind. As the chart shows, they promoted a total of 741 people to officer for the first time during 1970. Of that number, 47 or 6.3% were white women. Twenty-five or 3.4% were minority males. None were minority women.

FIRST-TIME PROMOTIONS TO OFFICER-SIX BANKS
1970

Total Promotions	741
Males	
Total	694
White	669
Minority	25
Females	
Total	47
White	47
Minority	0

At the individual banks, white men received from 87.5% to 96.0% of all such promotions during that same year. Minority women, as already noted, received none of them.

White women fared best at National Bank of Washington, where they received 12.5% of the promotions, worst at Continental Illinois with 3.3%. At most, minority males accounted for 4.9% at Manufacturers Hanover; at First Pennsylvania, none were promoted to the officer level for the first time during the year.

PERCENTAGE OF FIRST-TIME PROMOTIONS
1970

Bank	Total	Males White	Min.	Total	Females White	Min.
Chase Manhattan	96.0%	93.3%	2.7%	4.0%	4.0%	0.0%
Continental Illinois	96.7	92.3	4.4	3.3	3.3	0.0
Manufacturers Hanover	91.3	86.4	4.9	8.7	8.7	0.0
Citizens & Southern	89.6	88.1	1.5	10.4	10.4	0.0
First Pennsylvania	91.7	91.7	0.0	8.3	8.3	0.0
National Bank of Washington	87.5	83.3	4.2	12.5	12.5	0.0

Testing

In 1968, Secretary of Labor Willard Wirtz issued an order[1] which promised to ameliorate employment discrimination by prohibiting biased, unrealistic, or irrelevant job testing. Many examinations had proved culturally skewed in favor of middle-class white males. Others called for knowledge unrelated to the demands of the actual work or failed to predict the quality of on-the-job performance. Some employers set higher cut-off points, or passing grades, than necessary.

Secretary Wirtz's order required firms doing business with the Federal government, including banks, to standardize "any paper-and-pencil or performance measure used to judge qualifications for hire, transfer, or promotion." The order specified that examinations must be given either to every applicant or to none and that they must be validated-- i.e. shown to be predictive or meaningfully related to the job in question. Professional, technical, and managerial positions were exempted.

Four years after its issuance, the order has yet to be implemented. Part of the delay is due to the fact that the Office of Federal Contract Compliance and the Equal Employment Opportunity Commission did not issue guidelines for employment selection procedures--which include testing-- until 1970. These agencies bear prime responsibility for carrying out the provisions of the Civil Rights Act, and Cabinet departments need their guidelines in order to determine whether Federal contractors within their jurisdiction are in compliance. Without guidelines, therefore, Treasury could not ascertain whether banks were following proper procedures.

Further delay has resulted from the costly, time-consuming nature of validation. The order requires that it be conducted by means of generally accepted procedures, like those outlined by the American Psychological Association, and a psychologist's expertise is needed. Because jobs are fairly uniform throughout the banking industry, the E.E.O.C. and O.F.C.C. have granted the American Bankers Association's request that it be permitted to explore the possibility of industry-wide, rather than bank-by-bank, validation. According to the director of the A.B.A.'s Personnel Administration and Management Development Committee, George B. Ward, several consulting psychologists have submitted what are, in effect, bids for development of an industry-wide validation model. A decision on whether to develop a new test or to use an existing one was pending at the time of C.E.P.'s interview with Mr. Ward.

Neither E.E.O.C. nor O.F.C.C. seeks to end the use of tests because other methods are felt to be even less objective. Employers who use no examinations at all must show that their other procedures are valid and fair. Section 1607.13 of E.E.O.C.'s testing guidelines states that selection techniques other than tests

> ...may be improperly used so as to have the effect of
> discriminating against minority groups. Such techniques
> include, but are not restricted to, unscored or casual
> interviews and unscored application forms. Where there
> are data suggesting employment discrimination, the[employer]
> may be called upon to present evidence concerning the
> validity of his unscored procedures, as well as any
> tests which may be used...

Only four sample banks have validated their tests: Philadelphia National, Continental Illinois, National of Washington, and Northern Trust. Others claim to be doing little or no testing for entry-level positions. George Ward informs C.E.P. that: "Confusion was caused by the government's vacillating over a period of years, and the desire to avoid the charge of discrimination has led many companies, including banks, to discontinue the use of tests altogether."

Meanwhile, the Treasury Department's compliance section has been disregarding validation when determining whether a bank is obeying Federal law. Program specialist David Gottlieb and assistant director Inez Lee confirmed that compliance officers make no inquiries on the subject. Ms. Lee said, "As far as I know, we aren't telling them anything." And Mr. Gottlieb said that "the area is still blurry."

If validation does become a reality, employers as well as employees should benefit. Corporations have been using expensive procedures and arbitrary cut-off scores without knowing the value of either. Sometimes the results have been counterproductive. For example, one New York City bank hired proof-machine operators on the basis of high test scores only to find later that these applicants were more likely to quit work within six months than those with low scores.[2]

Notes

[1] U.S. Department of Labor Order, Chapter 60-3 under Title 41.

[2] R. David Corwin, New Workers in The Banking Industry: A Minority Report (New York: New York University , 1970), p.63.

Blacks: The Image of Banking

Despite banks' avowals in annual reports that they are aggressively
seeking and employing minorities at all levels, the industry's image
in the black community remains negative. Blacks have traditionally
viewed the industry as one which refuses to hire them or to serve
their financial needs and which thereby prevents them from establishing
financial institutions of their own. The persistence of the negative
image helps explain banks' difficulties in recruiting significant
numbers of blacks for their executive-management training programs.

Several surveys have documented this image. In 1970, Louis Harris
Associates conducted 3,000 interviews for the Foundation for Full
Service Banks, a non-profit trade association whose membership includes
6,500 commercial banks. Four hundred four of the interviewees were
minority adults, and 59% of these respondents maintained that bankers
have little or no concern with helping the community.[1] The other 41%
felt that bankers are concerned with helping it, compared with 69%
of the whites interviewed.

In 1971, another study, involving 853 students at eight predominantly
black colleges and universities in the south, was conducted for the
American Bankers Association by the National Urban League. The average
annual income of the students' families was less than $7,000.[2] Respondents
were asked to rank various professions in order of preference. Banking
was the sixth choice, preferred by only 5.1% of the students. In
comparison, their other choices were:

businessman	35.0%
physician	10.9
government administrator	9.5
lawyer	8.5
engineer	5.6
college professor	4.0

The occupations of agency administrator, research scientist, judge,
politician, artist, and real estate dealer received less than 4.0% each.
The students were also asked why they thought banks recruit blacks.
Twenty per cent said that banks want to use their talents. But 80%
gave negative reasons, with 50% maintaining that recruitment was meant
to meet government quotas, 25% citing "window dressing," and 4%
attributing it to charity.

Black bankers, too, are suspicious of white banking. One, who
requested anonymity, told C.E.P. that white bankers became involved
in minority affairs only because of the riots of the 1960s. A high
A.B.A. official, who is white, agreed with that view. The black

banker goes on to say that in reality "the bastards won't move. [The black community needs] some more Rap Browns and Stokely Carmichaels."

The same official accuses the American Bankers Association of guile in connection with a management training program jointly run by the A.B.A. and the N.B.A. (See "Industry Associations.") For the past two years, the N.B.A. has increased the number of trainees. While the program was meant to enlarge the reservoir of black management personnel available to black banks, C.E.P.'s source charges that the N.B.A. knew that black banks could not absorb all the trainees and therefore hoped that these blacks would find work in white banks. To forestall that·possibility, he continues, the A.B.A. has decided to re-evaluate the program. Peter McNeish, director of the A.B.A.'s Urban Affairs Committee, confirms that the program is being re-evaluated. He states that the A.B.A. recognizes the need to prepare blacks for executive jobs in banks, especially in those of small and moderate size, but he points out that this particular program's purpose is to prepare blacks for work in minority banking and that its "track record" in such placements is worse this year than last. "We don't think either the N.B.A. or the A.B.A. can stand this sort of exposure. We're going to train to meet the needs of the minority [banking] community," he says.

Notes

1 Harris, op. cit., Vol. I, p.130.

2 American Banker, April 26, 1971.

Blacks: Minority Lending

While blacks constitute 11% of the population of the United States, they own less than 1% of the nation's business and control less than 6.5% of its personal income.[1] How this imbalance should be redressed is a matter of intense debate. Andrew F. Brimmer, an economist and the only black member of the Federal Reserve Board, is notable among those who argue that the concept of black economic development is illusory at best. Although he has recently assumed a more conciliatory position, Dr. Brimmer has asserted that "the most promising path of economic development for Negroes lies in full participation in an integrated economy," not in an economic strategy based on "separatism and segregation."[2] Dr. Brimmer has argued that even a successful black capitalism program would yield meager results. According to him, if the existing imbalance were completely corrected so that blacks owned 11% of all retail and service establishments--the areas in which their businesses are now concentrated--they would then employ only 11% of all blacks in the labor force.

Still, minority economic development has received the imprimatur of the Nixon Administration, and blacks themselves are talking increasingly of self-sufficiency as a route to social and political parity with whites. A black management consultant says, "Equality is related to economic power. This country is geared to businessmen. It is capitalistic. People who cannot produce for themselves are weak." A high-ranking member of a Chicago community economic development organization rebuts Dr. Brimmer more succinctly: "Bullshit," he says.

The natural focal point for aspiring black entrepreneurs is the banking industry, traditional supplier of credit to American business. Major banks, the Small Business Administration, and local community development agencies have embarked upon programs to lend money to blacks whose business proposals violate established criteria as to what constitutes a "bankable loan." Normally, a "bankable loan" is one made to a company or person possessing an easily-verifiable credit history, a substantial portion of the money needed to launch the enterprise, and prior managerial experience in the particular field; the borrower is also expected to maintain a compensating balance at the bank, in the form of a deposit, when the loan is made. Many minority entrepreneurs cannot meet these requirements.

Packaging Loan Requests

Minority entrepreneurs often package their requests for loans poorly, omitting part of the information the bank requires, or fail to even prepare such a request. Typically, a loan proposal will include: short biographies of the principals involved; income tax returns for several years; a marketing analysis; projected cash-flow statements; an itemization of the entrepreneur's net worth, e.g. savings, life insurance, automobiles, and houses; and copies of leases and insurance policies on any existing business.

Some banks will do much, or all, of the packaging themselves. Others rely completely on outside organizations, many of which are funded through government sources to provide such services. Major organizations of this kind include Bedford Stuyvesant Restoration, Inc., the Interracial Council for Business Opportunity, and the Puerto Rican Forum, all located in New York; the Inner City Business Improvement Forum (I.C.B.I.F.) in Detroit; and the Chicago Economic Development Corporation. A New York banker told the Council on Economic Priorities that the quality of packaging by outside agencies "ranges from the ridiculous to the sublime." Most bankers express satisfaction but hope that the quality of packaging will improve with the passage of time.

The American Bankers Association

The American Bankers Association encourages member banks to aid minority economic development. (See "Industry Associations.") It has set a $1.5 billion industry-wide goal for minority lending for the five years ending in 1975, and it tries to monitor these activities through its annual Urban and Community Affairs Survey.

The Small Business Administration

Minority loans are usually made with the aid of the Small Business Administration, an independent agency created by Congress in 1953. Since 1968, it has officially encouraged the maximum amount of minority lending by banks, as a result of the efforts of former S.B.A. director Howard Samuels and former Secretary of Commerce Maurice Stans.[3] The S.B.A. made 17,425 loans amounting to $864,200,000 in 1970, and 39% of these went to minority businesses. In 1971 it lent $1,290,300,000, 18% of which went to minorities, a substantial increase over the previous year in dollars and in numbers of loans. However, critics maintain that the S.B.A.'s effectiveness is limited by the amount of red tape involved and the length of time needed before a guarantee can be obtained.[4]

The S.B.A. guarantees loans granted by private banks. It does so under two programs, "7a" and "Economic Opportunity," which differ in the size of the loan permitted and the extent of the guarantee. Under 7a, the S.B.A. will guarantee up to 90% of a loan, to a $350,000 maximum, repayable by the individual to the bank over 15 years for construction loans and ten years for non-construction loans. The equity--i.e. the entrepreneur's own financial resources--is expected to equal the amount of the guarantee; but the S.B.A. says that this requirement is flexible and that the equity can be as little as 15% of the guarantee. "Economic Opportunity" loans (E.O.L.) have no equity requirement and can be guaranteed for as much as 100% of the dollar value, payable over 15 years. But the size of the loan is limited to $25,000. As its name implies, this program is limited to the "disadvantaged" businessman.

The S.B.A. will also grant loans, or "participate" with a bank in granting them, to entrepreneurs who have been refused loans by two banks. In these cases, the bank may not levy interest at a rate more than two points above prime or 8%, whichever is lower.[5]

All the sample banks reporting claim to be making "soft" or "watch" loans, i.e. loans to minority businesspeople who would not qualify under customary criteria.

The following table presents aggregate data for the three sample banks in each city as of February 29, 1972: the total number of loans, the dollar amounts, and the percent guaranteed by the S.B.A. under the 7a and E.O.L. programs. The chart has several weaknesses as an indicator of the extent to which banks in a particular city assist minority business. First, it does not reveal whether each of the three banks made an equal number of loans or lent equal amounts of money. Second, it reflects lending by banks which rely heavily on S.B.A. guarantees more accurately than that by others. For example, S.B.A. guarantees cover virtually all minority loans made by two Detroit banks but virtually none of those made by Chase Manhattan and Citizens and Southern. Third, the chart does not indicate the number of volume or loans covered by 7a, as opposed to E.O.L. The distinction is important because many banks have shifted away from 7a, with its 90% guarantee, to E.O.L., with its 100% guarantee. This shift, of course, further minimizes the bank's risk. More significantly, it may also indicate a lack of commitment to minority lending.

MINORITY LOANS
Guarantee and Participation

Business and Economic Opportunity Loan Programs
(as of February 29, 1972)

Banks	No. Loans Outstanding	Amount Approved by S.B.A. Total	S.B.A. Share
New York Chase Manhattan First National City Manufacturers Hanover	111	$ 5,598,200	$ 4,771.230
Chicago First National Continental Illinois Northern Trust Company	127	8,270,567	7,380,510
Philadelphia First Pennsylvania Philadelphia National Girard	291	9,622,300	7,830,605
District of Columbia Riggs American Security National of Washington	41	2,155,200	1,934,680
Detroit National Bank of Detroit Manufacturers National Detroit Bank & Trust	321	13,831,400	12,251,460
Atlanta Citizens & Southern First National Trust Company of Georgia	54	2,508,000	2,162,680

The next table shows similar data for the three-bank sample involvement in "participation" loans, as of February 29, 1972. At that time, none of the C.E.P. banks in New York or Chicago were involved with the S.B.A. in this program.

MINORITY LOANS
"Participation"
(as of February 29, 1972)

| Banks | No. Loans Outstanding | Amount Approved by S.B.A. | |
		Total	S.B.A. Share
Philadelphia First Pennsylvania Philadelphia National Girard	20	$2,380,000	$1,474,250
District of Columbia Riggs American Security National of Washington	1	175,000	131,250
Detroit National Bank of Detroit Manufacturers National Detroit Bank & Trust	1	25,000	12,500
Atlanta Citizens & Southern First National of Atlanta Trust Company of Georgia	4	324,200	234,850

A major disadvantage of S.B.A. programs is their requirement of a fixed amortization schedule, which may be unsuitable for businesses whose financial needs are seasonal.[6] Also, the S.B.A.'s equity requirement, no matter how small, may lie beyond the means of many minority businesspeople.

Minority Enterprise Small Business Investment Companies

S.B.A. loans and other lending activity by banks are supplemented by M.E.S.B.I.C.'s--Minority Enterprise Small Business Investment Companies. A M.E.S.B.I.C. is similar to an S.B.I.C. (Small Business Investment Company), which is a Federally-licensed, privately-owned company specializing in providing equity capital and long-term loans to small businesses. A M.E.S.B.I.C. differs from an S.B.I.C. in two ways: it is legally restricted to making loans to businesses whose ownership and management are at least 50% minority; and it must have a "strong parent" in each instance--i.e. a bank, corporation, or other source which will pay overhead costs. Any group of private citizens or corporations can form a M.E.S.B.I.C. by (1) raising $150,000, the minimum amount of capital required; (2) agreeing to serve as the strong parent; and (3) securing a license from the S.B.A. For every dollar of capital raised, the S.B.A. will buy two dollars of long-term debentures, thus leveraging the total amount of money available to three times the initial investment.

65

By obtaining equity capital through a M.E.S.B.I.C., the minority entrepreneur may be able to obtain an S.B.A. loan for which she or he would not otherwise qualify. Also, while banks seldom make loans for a term of more than five years, M.E.S.B.I.C.s must make loans of at least five years' duration. The minority business therefore faces smaller loan payments spread over a longer time span. When a M.E.S.B.I.C. provides equity capital, there may be no payments at all; instead, the M.E.S.B.I.C. receives a percentage of the business' profits.

Critics find serious weaknesses in M.E.S.B.I.C.s. Professors Richard S. Rosenbloom and John K. Shank of Harvard Business School have written:

> Successful M.E.S.B.I.C.s would probably require a minimum capitalization of $3-5 million to be able to average out losses and cover overhead.* Typically, if an S.B.I.C. has been successful, it is because the company was able to withstand heavy losses suffered in most investments by "striking it rich" on a golden few. But a broad capital base is needed to obtain the necessary diversification of the investment portfolio and the time to wait patiently for the winners to take off. M.E.S.B.I.C.s will find it hard to gain diversity in view of their limited capital and in view of the fact that their dealings are restricted mainly to poor communities.
> ....
>
> The second major weakness that derives from smallness of scale is the limitation imposed on the size of loans or investments a M.E.S.B.I.C. can make. By statute, any S.B.I.C. must limit its total commitment in any one venture to not more than 20% of its (the S.B.I.C.'s) private invested capital. Thus, if a M.E.S.B.I.C. is capitalized at $150,000, it cannot commit more than $30,000 to any one business.
>
> This requirement limits, if it does not eliminate, the possibility of a M.E.S.B.I.C. becoming involved in business ventures of significant scale. Such limitation encourages tokenism via the Mom and Pop businesses and does nothing to encourage the development of businesses with real economic clout.[7]

These criticisms are underscored by the recent failure of Arcata, the much-publicized California M.E.S.B.I.C. which was organized in 1968 and capitalized at $300,000, and which has sustained losses of half a million dollars.

---

* Elsewhere, Professors Rosenbloom and Shank set $1 million as the minimum capitalization for success.

Ten of the 18 sample banks participate in M.E.S.B.I.C.s. (Information about uncooperative banks was obtained from the O.M.B.E. and other sources.) Chase Manhattan and Manufacturers Hanover belong to a consortium of banks taking part in one, and Northern Trust and Continental Illinois, along with other Chicago banks, are involved in another. Both are capitalized at $1 million. The three Philadelphia sample banks, First Pennsylvania, Girard, and Philadelphia National, are among the sponsors of a $750,000 M.E.S.B.I.C. The three Washington banks, Riggs, American Security and Trust, and National Bank of Washington, are part of a group of banks in still another capitalized at $168,000.

C.E.P. attempted to get information about lending from several of the outside service agencies. Two were willing to release some in exchange for a promise of anonymity. The rest refused comment on any basis and implied that even anonymous comment might jeopardize their ability to borrow funds for their clients. This reluctance to discuss minority lending is accentuated by interlocking relationships: in some cities, these organizations' boards of directors include top bankers, while in at least one instance, an organization's president sits on the board of a bank.

The agencies do claim that sample banks and others are not active enough in minority economic development, especially since most loans carry a 90% guarantee so that the bank will lose little if the business fails. The director of economic development at one New York City firm says that his organization has had to guarantee the remaining 10% before a certain bank would agree to make loans. Service agencies also state that banks are unwilling to finance large enterprises, preferring small economic units with minimum financial exposure for themselves. The enterprises financed are thus too small to have a significant impact on the minority community, either by creating more jobs or by stemming the outward flow of capital into white banks.

Monitoring Soft Loans

A number of sample banks declined to provide information about their minority lending activities on the grounds that they themselves were not sure what these were. If such programs deviate from the paradigmatic model of commercial lending, then a bank ought to monitor them closely. A proper analysis of soft loans would include the following:

--length of time the program has been in existence;

--number and dollar value of loans granted;

--total value of outstanding loans;

--amounts of money "charged off";

--dollar per cent of delinquent loans;

--per cent of re-lending;

--extent of use of S.B.A. and other guarantees and a clear
distinction between 7a and E.O.L. loans;

--number and dollar value of loans in manufacturing, retail, service, wholesale, and other areas;

--debt-equity ratios used;

--comparison of successful and unsuccessful enterprises;

--demands of soft loans on the time of bank staff, compared with demands of equivalent number and dollar value of regular loans.

Notes

[1] New York Times, January 10, 1972.

[2] American Banker, December 30, 1969.

[3] Joseph H. Hafkenschiel, Minority Economic Development: An Examination of Small Business Administration Programs, unpublished MBA thesis, University of California, March 1970.

[4] Ibid. Also New York Times, June 23, 1971.

[5] The prime rate is the rate of interest banks charge their best customers.

[6] Repayment of principal loaned.

[7] Richard S. Rosenbloom and John K. Shank, "Let's Write Off MESBICs," Harvard Business Review, September-October 1970, p.94.

Women: Maternity Policies

Because maternity policies have been a source of employment discrimination, the Equal Employment Opportunity Commission recently issued guidelines on the subject which define maternity as a "temporary disability" instead of a "condition." [1] The definition means that insurance benefits and sick leave provisions apply to pregnant women. It also means that banks and other employers may not require a woman to begin a maternity leave at a given stage of pregnancy, to remain on leave for a specified period following childbirth, or, indeed, to take any leave at all. Instead, the matter is left to the worker and her doctor. A bank may require a letter from the doctor declaring her physically fit, but it may not insist that she be examined by its own physician. Employees who voluntarily take leaves need not be restored to their former jobs on their return, but the new work must be "comparable" to the old and seniority must not be affected.

The guidelines are used by all Cabinet departments, including Treasury. However, they do not have the force of law, and there are no penalties for ignoring them. Inez Lee, assistant director of the compliance section, has indicated that many insurance companies are prepared to fight the new provisions. She also told the Council on Economic Priorities that she knew of "no recalcitrant bankers refusing to conform" to them. But she did not explain how the Equal Opportunity Program's small staff--estimated by one official at 20 people-has obtained that information from all 14,000 commercial banks since tne guidelines took effect in April of 1972.

At the time of the C.E.P. interviews, sample banks' maternity policies varied. Most respondents said that pregnant employees could continue working as long as they wished, provided that they presented written authorization from a doctor. One exception, Continental Illinois, required those who wanted to work during the last trimester to be examined by the bank's doctor; it justified this policy on the grounds that many minority employees at Continental do not receive adequate medical care on their own. All banks claimed that a woman was sure to find her old job or a comparable one waiting on her return from a leave.

The stage of pregnancy at which women were forced to leave work and the length of the leaves permitted afterward are listed below. Chase Manhattan, First Pennsylvania, Manufacturers National of Detroit, First National City, Continental Illinois, Citizens & Southern, and National Bank of Washington allowed six months off after childbirth. Other varied, with Manufacturers Hanover permitting six months' leave counted from the date of departure and National of Detroit requiring women to leave three months before delivery and return within three months after it.

MATERNITY POLICIES

Bank	Leave Commences	Leave Extends To:
American Security & Trust	Data Refused	Data Refused
Chase	Anytime with M.D. approval	6 months after birth
Citizens & Southern	Anytime with M.D. approval	6 months after birth
Continental Illinois	Anytime with Bank M.D. approval	6 months after birth
Detroit Bank & Trust	Data Refused	Data Refused
First National Bank Atlanta	Data Refused	Data Refused
First National Bank Chicago	End of 7th month	3 months after birth
First National City	Anytime with M.D. approval	6 months after birth or date of adoption
First Pennsylvania	End of 7th month	6 months after birth
Girard	Data Refused	Data Refused
Manufacturers Hanover	Anytime with M.D. approval	6 months after date of departure
Manufacturers National	End of 6th month	6 months after birth
National Bank of Detroit	End of 6th month	3 months after birth
National Bank of Washington	Anytime with M.D. approval	6 months after birth
Northern Trust	Anytime with M.D. approval	4 months after birth
Philadelphia National Bank	Anytime with M.D. approval	3 months after birth
Riggs	Data Refused	Data Refused
Trust Company of Georgia	Data Refused	Data Refused

A number of women insisted to C.E.P. that banks discriminate regardless of their stated policies. One said that she had felt compelled to keep her pregnancy secret as long as possible. Another recounted with relish that she had inadvertently foiled her bank's restrictions by working right through her ninth month because her doctor had estimated the date of delivery inaccurately. Another alleged that a bank which officially prohibited dismissals because of pregnancy fired employees anyway. Some workers scoffed at assurances that women who took leaves would find their original jobs or comparable ones waiting, and their seniority unimpaired, when they came back.

These comments could not be individually substantiated, but they were common enough to indicate that maternity can in fact occasion discrimination, whatever a bank's formal policy.

Notes

[1] Rules and Regulations, Federal Register, Vol. 37, No. 66, Sect. 1604.10 (Washington: April 5, 1972), p. 6837.

Women: Legal Challenges

Several significant challenges to sex discrimination by banks are now underway.

Women's Equity Action League

One is the class action filed with the Treasury Department by the Women's Equity Action League, a three-year old organization with chapters in 25 states. In October 1971, W.E.A.L. charged 27 Dallas banks with violating Executive Order 11246. (None of these banks is included in the study because Dallas ranks fourteenth in the nation in black population.) Specifically, it maintained that the banks took longer to promote female employees to the executive level than males; that they paid women less than men for the same work; and that many fired women upon learning that they had become pregnant while others forced them to leave work at a given stage of pregnancy and still others "moved them into the back room."

In January 1972, the Treasury Department sent eight men to conduct compliance reviews in Dallas. According to _Newsweek_, several of the banks promoted women to vice-presidencies or added them to their boards of directors the day before the Treasury representatives arrived. The men reviewed 20 banks in four days, then returned to Washington. In accordance with Treasury policy, the Department has declined to inform W.E.A.L. of the results of the review, nor has the organization heard any other word from the Department since January. The Council on Economic Priorities asked the highest-ranking woman in Treasury's compliance section, Inez Lee, about W.E.A.L.'s activities. Ms. Lee said, "Oh those ladies. They do upset me." Ms. Lee added that a lot of female employees at Dallas banks "think of their jobs as second jobs" and "are not interested in becoming officers because if they were they might have to travel on the spur of the moment."

W.E.A.L. also complained to the Equal Employment Opportunity Commission, but again has received no reply. Weary of the unresponsiveness of two Federal agencies, W.E.A.L. now plans to ask a third—the Justice Department—to file a class action suit. The group has also sued several Ohio banks and may sue in New York, as well.

Beverly Wadsworth and First National City

The protagonist in another major challenge is Beverly Wadsworth, who was graduated from Harvard _cum laude_ and who worked at First National City Bank in New York from October 1968 through August 1970. In response to her complaint, the New York State Division of Human Rights has filed suit on her behalf, charging that the bank and two of its officers discriminated against her by placing her in   training leading to personal, rather than commercial, lending and then by twice recommending that she be transferred from commercial lending to investment research. The suit also charges that she was discriminated against in regard to the nature of her initial job and in regard to rating reports, promotions, salary, and job responsibility and authority.

Before she joined the Citibank staff, Ms. Wadsworth explicitly expressed a desire to work in commercial lending in conversations with several bank officials and in a letter to a senior vice president. Ms. Wadsworth charges that the bank deceived her by indicating that she was being placed in a training program leading to commerical lending. In fact, three training programs then existed in the Metropolitan Division: (a) college training, for "outstanding graduates of colleges or graduate schools recruited...as potential members of senior management;" (b) platform management training, which prepared people mainly for work at branches, often at the officer level, with duties entailing "general supervision, loans, opening and closing of accounts, [and the direction of branch]activities...;"1 and (c) credit management, which was similar to platform management but was meant for people with less experience.2 Despite Ms. Wadsworth's educational background and several years' business experience, she was assigned to this last program, which has since been discontinued.

After three months' training, Ms. Wadsworth was made a credit analyst, a job which she subsequently described as "back-up work not involving customer contact and supporting the men in her office." On three occasions she complained to her supervising officer about not having been assigned any accounts; once she was told in reply that "there was nobody else to do [my]work." After she complained directly to the vice president in charge of all mid-Manhattan regional centers, she was given the title of official assistant, but was not given account responsibility. The following month, July 1969, her first account was delegated to her; in October, she was given a second one. The next March, she was made an account manager. In comparison, the complaint alleges, a certain male employee who began work as a college trainee two months after Ms. Wadsworth did had 24 accounts by the time she had been given one. Ms. Wadsworth claims that the disparity resulted from the bank's desire "to keep me...doing routine paperwork and odd jobs to support the men."

Ms. Wadsworth's department had no female officers, and only 14 of its 166 non-clerical personnel were women. Ms. Wadsworth maintains that an examination of recruitment, training, and promotion statistics would reveal "massive prejudice in favor of the males." C.E.P. can neither support nor refute this contention because Citibank declined to supply statistical data despite repeated requests.

When Citibank was reorganized in January 1970, Ms. Wadsworth was transferred to the Personal Banking Group, a retail area; after vigorous protests, she was transferred back into commercial lending. At the time of the reorganization, no women had account responsibility in the Commercial Banking Group.

74

The complaint also deals with the granting of signing powers, which involved a salary increase and were a prerequisite for promotion to officer. Two male trainees were given this authority, but Ms. Wadsworth was not. When she objected, a Citibank vice president told her that "women should not be out at night and should therefore not be promoted to a position where they would have to sign documents and seal the branch at the end of each day." The same executive told her that women are not good at getting new business and that the only reasons for promoting women are the 1964 Civil Rights Act and the fact that men are less likely to lose their tempers when complaining to a female employee.

Finally, the complaint alleges discriminatory use of rating systems. Ms. Wadsworth maintains that the senior officer in her branch specified that her performance appraisals not be discussed with her, as they were with other employees. She was rated twice while at Citibank. Both times, she says, she had to ask to see the results instead of being shown them automatically as bank policy dictated. Both times the ratings were high. Yet both reports suggested that she be transferred to another department; according to Ms. Wadsworth, the suggestions were made because the bank did not want women in commercial lending.

Public hearings in the case were completed in June 1972. Attorneys for both sides are preparing final briefs, with an opinion expected from the hearing examiner by year's end.

The Bank of America Case

In still another attempt to make the machinery move, three employees of the International Division of the Bank of America in San Francisco have filed a complaint with E.E.O.C. and begun a class action in U.S. District Court. (Two of the three have since left the bank.) Kathleen E. Wells, Barbara Louise Sowers, and Kerstin Fraser went to E.E.O.C. in December 1970 and into court in March 1971, charging violations of Section 703 of Title VII of the 1964 Civil Rights Act in job classification, promotions, pay, recruitment, training, and other matters. (The Bank of America is not included in the sample because San Francisco, where its headquarters are located, ranks twenty-seventh in the nation in black population.) A summary of the accusations follows:

Jobs: Bank of America jobs are divided into 28 grades, and Mses. Wells, Sowers, and Fraser allege that most female employees are located in the lower ones. Grades numbered ten and above are considered managerial positions, and the lowest one which carries a corporate title, that of pro-assistant cashier, is seven.[3] At the bank's offices in San Francisco and Alameda counties, the higher the grade the more nearly all-male its personnel: 10-15, 16-19, and 20-28 are respectively 65.4%, 96.5%, and 100% male. The International Division has 848 employees, of whom 445 or 52.5% are female; however only 16 of them are in or above grade nine.[4] The median grade for women is

four, that for men 13. In 1971, 86% of the Division's officials and
managers and 23 of its 26 department supervisors were male.

Promotions: During the two years ending February 1971, only 4.9% of
the International Division's female employees were promoted to
managerial jobs as opposed to 31% of the males. Women constituted
57.6%* of the Division's staff but received only 18% of all
such promotions.[5] They also spent more than three times longer than
men in the bank's employ before rising to the management level--7.4
years compared with 2.3 years; and college-educated women waited
eight times longer than college-educated men.

Pay: The three plaintiffs charge that women receive lower starting
salaries and are also paid less than men for doing substantially equal
work. Median salaries in most of the upper grades are $10-$241/month
higher for men. And the bank is said to have discriminated against
women in regard to ratings, upon which pay increases largely depend.

Recruitment and Training: Until 1971, the bank did not recruit at any
women's colleges, And until then it excluded women from its training
programs for overseas management.

E.E.O.C.'s preliminary findings indicate that discrimination existed
as charged. The Commission found that the "predominance of women in
lower-level jobs [is] due in large part to [their] overt exclusion...
from management training program and to the exclusion of men from
consideration for clerical positions."[6] It also found that male
trainees received higher starting salaries in the two programs to which
women were admitted.

In addition, the findings showed that the bank's employment guide
prohibited sex discrimination yet tended to "perpetuate stereotypes."
For example, it used male pronouns when referring to job applicants
with college degrees and female pronouns when referring to potential
stenographers and typists. According to E.E.O.C., it also implied that
interviewers should question women more closely than men about marital
status and related matters. Furthermore, the guide warned interviewers
to "watch for...complaining about unfair treatment, excuses for failures,
or anti-establishment views" on the part of applicants.

The E.E.O.C. reviewed 376 randomly-chosen personnel applications and
found references to the secretarial skills of females but none to
those of males. The findings also quoted these comments, written by
a Bank of America recruiter who had interviewed a female college
graduate with an A-minus grade point average: "The worst personality
I've ever come in contact with, very defensive, abrasive type--almost
mean. Hates children--Women's Liber type---looks like a boy---very
offensive to me.....Do Not Hire.." Later, the same recruiter defined
a "Women's Liber type" as a woman who is "very defensive of the fact

---

*Payroll records as of Feb. 26, 1971, cited in E.E.O.C. Findings p.39
 Finding #193.

that she is a woman." And the Commission quoted a bank official as having referred to one of the two "lady" officers at its London branch as "a girl who's been with us for 31 years."

In response to the E.E.O.C. findings, the bank filed a 34-page rebuttal in March 1972. It contended: that progress has been made throughout the bank; that women constituted 22% of all officers by mid-1971; that employees are now recruited on predominantly female campuses; that women are currently enrolled in management training programs, although "with the understanding that they will not receive overseas assignments"; and that salaries in the International Division are comparable when "equalled by grade, performance, and time on assignment."

The Commission is now preparing final findings.

Three months after they went to E.E.O.C., Mses. Wells, Sowers, and Fraser went to court. The first judge in the case disqualified himself because he owned stock in the Bank of America. Two days after the suit was filed, the director of Treasury's compliance section, David Sawyer, praised the bank's affirmative action program for women and minorities at a news conference; at that time, the bank had no affirmative action program for women. The taking of depositions in the District Court suit began in October 1971 and is still in progress, having been slowed by the plaintiffs' lack of money. Their attorney, Barbara Phillips, recently helped establish a non-profit organization named the Women's Legal Defense Fund to solicit funds for litigation of women's employment cases.

After the Bank of America complaint was filed with E.E.O.C., but before the start of District Court proceedings, the Treasury conducted a compliance review of the bank, at the bank's request. The review was the first conducted there—although the Bank of America is the largest in the world. The results of the review have not been released.

In the words of The American Banker, a daily newspaper for the banking industry, the Bank of America case

> has wide significance. The wealth of information and detailed analysis contained in the E.E.O.C. and B.ofA. documents is likely to form a case-book study of job discrimination disputes for the banking industry and is almost certain to be referred to where other, similar, cases arise in the future. Most important, observers stress, many of the practices investigated have been ones which, until now, have not been considered potentially discriminatory. The scope of the investigation, then, has made clear to the industry the extent to which banks around the country may be held answerable to the E.E.O.C.[7]

Notes

[1] Corwin, op. cit., p.16.

[2] First National City Bank memorandum, "Credit Management," presented as testimony in the case of Beverly Wadsworth vs. First National City Bank et al.

[3] District Director's Findings of Fact, Kathleen E. Wells et al. vs. Bank of America National Trust and Savings Association, Case No. YSF2-050 (San Francisco, Equal Employment Opportunity Commission, no date), p.2.

[4] Ibid., Finding #134, p.29.

[5] Ibid., Finding #193, p.39.

[6] Ibid., Finding #148, p.31.

[7] American Banker, March 6, 1972.

Part 3

Bank Profiles

AMERICAN SECURITY AND TRUST COMPANY
Fifteenth Street and Pennsylvania Avenue, N.W., Washington, D.C.,
    20013 (202/624-4000)

Number of Employees: 1,208
Number of Branches: 30

	1971	1970
Deposits (in millions of dollars as of December 31st):	$735.2	$695.4
Per Share Net Operating Earnings:	$2.18	$2.08

	U.S.A.	City	C.E.P. Sample
1970 Rank by Deposits:	91	2	17

President: Joseph W. Barr
Chairman: Robert C. Baker
Board of Directors: Alvin L. Aubinoe
                     William R. Biggs
                     George B. Burrus
                     James F. Collins
                     Lloyd H. Elliott
                     George M. Elsey
                     Joe Hume Gardner
                     Gordon Gray
                     Edwin K. Hoffman
                     R.L. Ireland, III
                     Howard W. Kacy
                     William T. Leith
                     George C. McGhee
                     William H. Moore
                     Paul H. Nitze
                     Thorton W. Owen
                     Gustave Ring
                     S. Dillon Ripley
                     Andrew M. Saul
                     John W. Sweeterman
                     James F. Willert
                     Stanley Woodward

81

American Security and Trust was rated Poor because the bank declined to participate in any way. The questionnaire and related material were sent to Joseph Barr, president. His office turned the request over to Charles Gasquely, vice president for personnel, who first informed C.E.P. that he was preparing a memo on the subject for Mr. Barr's attention and later said that American Security and Trust would not participate in the study because the bank does not release such information to private groups. Mr. Barr subsequently asked that a second copy of the request be sent him so that the decision to withhold information might be reconsidered. The duplicate material was sent on October 14, 1971. No further word was heard.

A Treasury Department official has told C.E.P. that 38% of all American Security and Trust employees are members of minority groups. In March 1972, a source at the bank indicated that American Security and Trust: (1) has one black officer and one female assistant treasurer; (2) has seven management trainees, including two blacks and two women; and (3) has no formal minority economic development program and supposedly "discourages" such lending. The same source makes the unsupported allegation that Robert Baker, chairman of the board, is considered "anti-minority" and "anti-woman."

CHASE MANHATTAN BANK, N. A.

One Chase Manhattan Plaza, New York, New York 10005 (212/552-2222)

Number of Employees: 25,154 (Chase Manhattan Corp.)
Number of Branches: 158 (Domestic)

	1971	1970
Deposits (in billions of dollars as of December 31st):	$20.4	$21.3
Net Operating Earnings Per Share:	$4.43	$3.85

	U.S.A.	City	C.E.P. Sample
1970 Rank by Deposits:	2	1	1

President: Herbert P. Patterson
Chairman: David Rockefeller
Board of Directors: David Rockefeller
                      Herbert P. Patterson
                      George A. Roedee, Jr.
                      Willard C. Butcher
                      Lenor F. Loree II*
                      Robert O. Anderson
                      John T. Connor
                      C.W. Cook
                      J. Richardson Dilworth
                      Patricia Roberts Harris
                      William R. Hewlett
                      J.K. Jamieson
                      Frederick R. Kappel
                      Ralph Lazarus
                      Robert D. Lilley
                      John H. Loudon
                      Jeremiah Millbank, Jr.
                      Charles F. Myers, Jr.
                      James A. Perkins
                      Richard R. Shinn*
                      J. Henry Smith
                      Whitney Stone
                      John E. Swearingen
                      Thomas A. Wood
*Bank Director Only

83

However far we go, I don't think we can ever give up our
principal activity of lending money to our principal customers,
but I certainly don't think we have exhausted the possibilities of what we can do. It seems clear to me that the entire
structure of our society is being challenged and unless
banks and other businesses take greater interest in what
happens to society, there's a real possibility that our system
will be radically changed or abandoned, and I can't see that
that would be constructive.

--David Rockefeller, Chairman
1971 annual report

Chase Manhattan is the largest bank in New York, the largest in the
sample, and the second largest in the nation, behind the Bank of
America. Its main office and 158 branches employ a total of 21,000
people.

It was one of the first banks to agree to participate in the study,
and it was one of two whose cooperation was Very Good.

Employment

Chase has both female and minority representation on its board of
directors; First Pennsylvania is the only other sample bank of which
that is true. Thomas A. Wood and Patricia Roberts Harris, both of
whom are black, were elected in 1971 and 1972, respectively. In
addition, one woman and three minority people are full vice presidents.

The composition of the bank's entire work force includes 30.2%
minorities, and the composition of the officials and managers category
includes 6.8% minorities. The distribution of minority workers includes
89.5% in office and clerical jobs and another 3.4%, mostly male, in
official and managerial positions. 54.6% of the total staff and 14.7%
of the officials and managers are female. 90.4% of all women do office
and clerical work; another 4.0% are executives. The distribution of
minority women is 96.3% office-clerical and 1.0% official-managerial.

See Table 1.

Affirmative Action

Chase adopted an affirmative action program in 1964, before any other
sample bank. Information about it is disseminated internally in much
the same manner used by other banks--through the management policy
guide, the staff handbook, and a signed letter from the chairman and
president of the board in Chase's newspaper. Executive vice president
William Bateman has charge of personnel. The compliance officer is
Warren Conrad, a second vice president who reports to Paul Shaw, vice
president and director of employee relations. At the time of the
Council on Economic Priorities' initial interview in the Fall of 1971,
Mr. Conrad indicated that the affirmative action program was being
re-examined with an eye toward utilizing it for a "task analysis" or
"skills inventory" of personnel by means of a computer. At that same
time, Chase had no separate program for women, but by August 1972 the
bank said that it had begun one in compliance with Revised Order 4.

Table 1

OCCUPATIONS	MALE EMPLOYEES					FEMALE EMPLOYEES					TOTAL ALL EMPLOYEES
	Total Males	Minority Groups				Total Females	Minority Groups				
		NEGRO	ORIENTAL¹	AMERICAN INDIAN¹	SPANISH AMERICAN¹		NEGRO	ORIENTAL¹	AMERICAN INDIAN¹	SPANISH AMERICAN¹	
OFFICIALS AND MANAGERS	2660	74	-12-		63	457	46	-5-		13	3117
PROFESSIONALS	1501	67	-19-		72	457	28	-8-		11	1958
TECHNICIANS	228	33	--		32	101	23	-2-		4	329
SALES WORKERS	114	1	--		1	41	2	--		-	155
OFFICE AND CLERICAL	4579	1027	-81-		598	10336	3119	-115-		735	14915
CRAFTSMEN (Skilled)	85	5	-2-		8	10	3	--		0	95
OPERATIVES (Semiskilled)	84	15	--		3	23	4	--		0	107
LABORERS (Unskilled)	-	-	--		-	-	-	--		-	-
SERVICE WORKERS	293	81	-1-		19	13	4	-1-		0	306
TOTAL	9544	1303	-115-		796	11438	3229	-131-		763	20982

85

Recruiting

Like the other New York sample banks, Chase recruits extensively on the campus. It visited 63 schools in 1971. Eleven of these were predominantly black, and none was predominantly female. In 1972, Chase became the only sample bank in the city to visit Barnard, but the college's placement director and the two or three students interviewed indicated afterward that the white male recruiter had seemed to be on-campus under duress. The recruiting team consists of three full-time and 60 part-time people, including three women and three minority group members.

29% of all college graduates hired in both 1970 and 1971 were women. Blacks represented 5.2% in 1970 and 3.4% in 1971.

	TOTAL		BLACK		FEMALE	
	# Colleges	# Hires*	# Colleges	# Hires*	# Colleges	# Hires*
1971	63	324	11	11**	0	94
1970	73	480	11	25	0	138
1969	86	581	10	N/A	0	N/A

* Includes all holders of college degrees.
** To date of interview.

Testing

Testing procedures were being re-evaluated at the time of the interview.

Training

Chase has one of the larger, more centralized management training efforts among sample banks. The Global Credit Training Program prepares future lending officers by means of a highly structured program lasting about 24 months and emphasizing formal, in-bank course instruction as well as on-the-job learning. Six to nine months before graduation, each credit analyst is assigned to a Community Economic Development (--i.e. minority--) loan, which she or he continues to follow after the completion of training. Thus all Global Credit trainees acquire experience in handling minority business transactions.

Chase's 1971 annual report defines Global Credit as the bank's "principal source of officers." The program's composition is therefore an instructive indicator of Chase's attempts to upgrade minorities and women. In 1970, women accounted for 8.6% of all trainees. Blacks constituted 5.7%--5.5% of it male. Despite the large number of Hispanic Americans in the New York City labor force, no Spanish-surnamed men or women have yet participated.

	TOTAL		BLACK		HISPANIC		OTHER		WHITE	
	M	F	M	F	M	F	M	F	M	F
1971	183*		17*				data refused			
1970	159	15	9	1	0		0	0	150	14
1969	109				data refused					

* Chase did not provide a breakdown by sex.

First Time Promotions to Officer

In 1970, 4.0% of all employees promoted to officer for the first time
were white females and 2.9% minority males. Only one minority woman
received such a promotion during 1968-70.

	TOTAL		BLACK		HISPANIC		OTHER		WHITE	
	M	F	M	F	M	F	M	F	M	F
1970	314	13	2	0	4	0	3*	0	305	13
1969	296	12	4	0	3	1	0	0	289	11
1968	235	12	3	0	0	0	3**	0	229	12

* Oriental
**2 Oriental, 1 American Indian

Not long ago, the bank made an in-house study of the time its employees
spent on the staff before becoming officers. According to an unofficial
source, it showed that women waited an average of 15 years, compared
with six for men. Chase did not publicize the results.

Ratings

Employees' performance is rated annually, and official policy calls
for the workers to see and sign their reports.

Maternity

A pregnant woman may continue work as long as she wishes provided she
has signed authorization from her personal physician. Maternity
leaves can extend up to six months after childbirth.

Minority Lending

Chase spends more money advertising its economic development program
than some sample banks grant in actual soft loans. Full-page color
advertisements whose cost runs in the "high six figures" appear
regularly in publications like Time, Business Week, and the Wall Street
Journal. Management says the ads account for Chase's entire "public
service advertising" budget and are intended primarily to stimulate
minority lending by other banks.

Chase's soft loan program is probably the most highly organized and monitored one in the study. In contrast to most other banks, Chase has a clear idea of the amount of money in its Community Economic Development program (C.E.D.),the extent of the losses incurred, the nature of the businesses being funded, and the percentages guaranteed by the Small Business Administration and other agencies. Moreover, it is the only bank to indicate that officials who oversee these loans are held responsible for losses attributable to "inadequate follow-up and supervision."

C.E.D. was established in 1969. It has a nine-member staff headed by a full vice president, Lawrence Toal, and including five experienced loan officers. Loans commonly originate at one of the branches. They must be genuinely "unbankable" and must benefit a disadvantaged area by "creating new job opportunities, expanding community ownership, increasing the inflow or capital, or enhancing cultural and educational opportunities."

In the initial stages of the loan process, C.E.D. assigns a credit analyst from Global Credit Training to do the basic financial "legwork." C.E.D. keeps duplicates of all records and does the overall monitoring, handling marketing studies, securing outside equities and guarantees when necessary, and providing managerial and technical assistance. It also meets with the prospective entrepreneur and with the branch manager who will make the loan; the meeting is considered important because it often provides the only indication of the applicant's ability and character in the absence of documentary evidence.

Over a three-year period, the average dollar size of individual loans has increased from $25,000 to $61,000. S.B.A. guarantees increased from 13% to 23%, but Chase's use of them is nonetheless the second-lowest among sample banks.

	Gross Value (in millions)	Number Loans	Per Cent Guaranteed
1971	$2.1(6 months)	34	23%
1970	$5.7	99	16%
1969	$2.0	77	13%

The dollar percentage of S.B.A. guarantees is low, Mr. Toal says, because the agency's insistence upon a strict amortization schedule restricts the kind of loans Chase can make, particularly to businesses requiring a line of credit, an essential instrument for many seasonal enterprises and manufacturing operations with a high level of out-standing accounts receivable.

More loans with a larger dollar amount have been granted in the service area--to retail businesses like dry cleaning, auto repair, and shoe repair--than in any other category. However, while transactions in the manufacturing area represent only 11% of the number of loans made, they account for 28% of the total dollar value.

	Service	Retail	Manu-facturing	Con-struction	Other
Per Cent Loans	.40	.36	.11	.04	.09
Per Cent Dollar	.34	.18	.28	.08	.12

Chase has incurred a loss of 5.2% of net volume, 4.0% of it in the first $1.5 million. Even though net loss relative to dollar amount has been greater in the smaller loans, Mr. Toal does not object to the financing of "Ma and Pa" businesses, because they can "improve the quality of service to the community" and they have a positive "psychological impact." He is convinced that minority economic development creates customers for Chase and that the program's entire cost can be covered in three to five years when the C.E.D. portfolio matures.

Like Manufacturers Hanover, Chase belongs to a consortium of New York banks participating in a M.E.S.B.I.C. capitalized at $1 million.

CITIZENS & SOUTHERN BANK OF ATLANTA, GEORGIA

99 Annex, Atlanta, Georgia 30399 (404/588-2121)

Number of Employees: 2607 (1971)
Number of Branches: 37 (Atlanta Only)

	1971	1970
Deposits (in billions of dollars as of December 31st):	$1.6	$1.4
Per Share Net Operating Earnings:	$1.69	$1.69

	U.S.A.	City	C.E.P. Sample
1970 Rank by Deposits:	41	1	13

President: Richard L. Kattel
Chairman: J.F. Glenn - Vice Chairman: Mills B. Lane, Jr.
Board of Directors: G.H. Achenbach
                      A.P. Adams
                      B.A. Brown
                      J.D. Comer
                      J.N. Frazer
                      J.F. Glenn
                      J.A. Hall, III
                      L.G. Hardman, Jr.
                      Richard L. Kattel
                      E.W. Lane, Jr.
                      Mills B. Lane, Jr.
                      Harley Langdale, Jr.
                      J.R. Lientz
                      R.A. Maxwell
                      H.L. Smith
                      W.W. Spraque, Jr.
                      B.J. Tarbutton, Jr.
                      F.A. Townsend, Jr.
                      L.L. Gellerstedt, Jr.
                      H.S. Starks
                      R.P. Timmerman

Banks are the reservoir of a community's wealth, and that
wealth should be used to build the community constructively
and not through hand-outs. All of the money in the world
can't make a model city--only people can do that. Slums
can be changed when the people do something together with
the proper use of private capital instead of the government dole.

--Mills B. Lane, Jr., Vice Chairman

The cooperation of Citizens and Southern National, like that of Chase
Manhattan, is rated Very Good. It not only supplied relevant data
and permitted personal interviews but was the only sample bank to
provide a racial and sexual breakdown of executives authorized to
commit loans in excess of $1 million and the only one to invite
criticisms and suggestions from the Council on its 1972 affirmative
action goals and timetables. Citizens and Southern has offices
throughout the State; however, employment data for this report was
compiled from the main office in Atlanta.

Employment

Citizens and Southern National Bank's board of directors is 100%
white male. There are no black or female officers in the corporate
banking department, which handles commercial lending; nor are there
any black officers in trust management. The highest-ranking female is
an assistant vice president. The sole female branch manager retired
last year. The highest-ranking black is a male assistant vice president
and branch manager, and one black works in the Community Development
Corporation. No minority women are officers, but some are supervisors.

Minorities constitute 17.3% of the total staff and account for 1.4%
of all officials and managers; 1.0% of that 1.4% is male. 81.2% of
the minority employees are found in office and clerical jobs with a
substantial percentage, 15.8%, in blue collar and service positions.
Women constitute 60.8% of the entire staff and 15.9% of the officials
and managers. Yet 93.2% of them hold office and clerical jobs while
only 3.0% are executives; the 3.0% is largely white. 87.5% of the
minority females are at the clerical level, and another 11.3% are
below it.

See Table 2.

Lending Authority

Citizens and Southern is the only sample bank willing to break down
lending authority by race and sex. Of the 260 officers in Atlanta who may
commit loans in excess of $1 million without authorization from a super-
visor, 30 are women, two are black men, and one is an Hispanic male.
Therefore, 87.3% of the executives enjoying such status are white men,
8.0% are white women, 1.2% are minority men, and none are minority women.

Affirmative Action

Executive vice president Eugene Rackley, III is the bank's compliance
officer and also has charge of personnel. At the time of the C.E.P.

91

Table 2

OCCUPATIONS	MALE EMPLOYEES					FEMALE EMPLOYEES					TOTAL ALL EMPLOYEES
	Total Males	Minority Groups				Total Females	Minority Groups				
		NEGRO	ORIENTAL[1]	AMERICAN INDIAN[1]	SPANISH AMERICAN[1]		NEGRO	ORIENTAL[1]	AMERICAN INDIAN[1]	SPANISH AMERICAN[1]	
OFFICIALS AND MANAGERS	249	2	0	0	1	47	1	0	0	0	296
PROFESSIONALS	20	1	1	0	0	10	1	0	0	0	30
TECHNICIANS	23	5	0	0	0	7	2	0	0	0	30
SALES WORKERS	16	0	0	0	0	4	0	0	0	0	20
OFFICE AND CLERICAL	606	71	1	0	17	1476	262	0	0	16	2082
CRAFTSMEN (Skilled)	28	2	0	0	0	0	0	0	0	0	28
OPERATIVES (Semiskilled)	54	16	0	0	0	1	0	0	0	0	55
LABORERS (Unskilled)	—	—	—	—	—	—	—	—	—	—	—
SERVICE WORKERS	27	17	0	0	0	39	36	0	0	0	66
TOTAL	1023	114	2	0	18	1584	302	0	0	16	2607

interview, he was assisted by Don Rochow, who has since been reassigned
to the credit area. The affirmative action program was adopted in
January 1970 and is disseminated by means of the employee handbook and
personnel policy manual. It explicitly includes women.

Goals and objectives for both females and minorities have been formulated
and are to be effected by December 1972. They call for the addition of
members of both groups to departments from which they have been excluded
and for the upgrading of current employees by promotions. The goals
also call for greater use of minorities in clerical and teller positions,
where their numbers are considerably smaller than in other cities, and
for the addition of one minority group member to commercial lending.

Recruiting

The Citizens and Southern college recruiting team has 50 members, most
of them part-time, including four blacks and two females. The bank
visits black colleges like Alabama A. & M., Fiske, the Atlanta complex,
Howard, and Tuskegee, and recruits at Agnes Scott, a predominantly
female campus. The bank does not use professional full-time recruiters.

| | TOTAL | | BLACK | | FEMALE | |
	# Colleges	# Hires	# Colleges	# Hires	# Colleges	# Hires
1971	38	118	14	9	2	17
1970	44	132	12	9	1	6
1969	27	115	4	3	1	5

Nearly a third of all colleges visited in 1970 were largely black or
female, although students hired on black campuses accounted for only
6.8% of all college hires that year and students chosen at female
campuses for only 4.5%. Over a three-year period, hires on black
campuses constituted 5.8% of all college hires and those at women's
schools 7.7%. Like a number of other banks, Citizens and Southern
de-emphasizes recruitment of M.B.A.s, although Mr. Rahow asserts that
its $13-14,000 starting salaries for them are competitive.

Testing

Testing procedures have been validated for minority groups.

Training

Citizens and Southern's executive-management training process, the
Management Development Program, is an on-the-job program providing
experience in various departments and lasting until the trainee
becomes an officer, usually within 22-26 months. The program's
importance to employees seeking advancement is underscored by Citizens
and Southern's statement that "very few people are hired into the bank
at the officer level."

	TOTAL		BLACK		HISPANIC		OTHER		WHITE	
	M	F	M	F	M	F	M	F	M	F
1971	276	28	15	1	0	0	0	0	261	27
1970	258	12	9	0	1	0	0	0	248	12
1969	221	9	7	0	2	0	0	0	212	9
1968	201	4	4	0	2	0	0	0	195	4

The bank ranked last among the six providing data in affording training
opportunities to women and minorities. In 1970, only ten minority men--
nine blacks and one Hispanic American--participated, accounting for
3.7% of all trainees. In the same year, 12 white women were included--
4.4% of the total. Last year, women's participation grew to 9.2% and
that of minorities to 5.3%. The 1972 affirmative action goals call
for increasing minority group representation to 25 people or 10% of
the projected total of 240, but make no provision for a rise in the
number of female trainees.

First-Time Promotions to Officer

Compared with other reporting banks, Citizens and Southern has a good
record for first-time promotions of white women to officer and a poor
record for minorities of both sexes.

	TOTAL		BLACK		HISPANIC		OTHER		WHITE	
	M	F	M	F	M	F	M	F	M	F
1970	60	7	1	0	0	0	0	0	59	7
1969	76	4	0	0	3	0	0	0	73	4
1968	37	3	1	0	0	0	0	0	36	3

In 1970, 10.4% of all such promotions went to white women, a percentage
surpassed only by National of Washington. But minority males were
granted just 1.5% of them; only First Pennsylvania had a smaller per
cent. (No minority females rose to officer rank at any of the six banks
during 1970.) Citizens and Southern's goals and timetables call for
the promotion of at least five women to officer by the end of this
year.

Ratings

Employees up to the officer level are rated twice during their first
six months and semi-annually thereafter. They see and sign their
rating reports after discussion with their supervisors.

Supervisors rate workers on a scale of one (poor) to five (outstanding)
for: (a) sense of responsibility; (b) volume of work handled; (c)
initiative; (d) ability to learn; (e) ability to get along with co-
workers; (f) manner of speech; (g) ability to meet people at all
levels; and (h) capacity to inspire confidence in his decisions.

Department heads are required to answer the following questions:
1) Which performance or personal strengths exhibited by the employee
will be of the greatest value to his advancement? 2) Which areas
of performance or personal characteristics require improvement on the
current job assignment? 3) What steps and planned dates for completion
are assigned to help in accomplishing the required improvement? 4) What
skills or experience does the employee have which would be effectively
utilized on another job in the bank? 5) What position should the
employee fill after meeting current job requirements? 6) What additional development is required?

Employees themselves are asked for their opinions of the bank's
general policies and practices and for their thoughts on possible
transfers to other positions. The rating form also asks the supervisor
to comment on the employee's reaction to their discussion of the report.
Citizens and Southern is experimenting with a data bank meant to
consolidate information on each employee and thereby help identify those
who merit promotions.

Maternity

For a year or more, the bank's maternity policy has allowed pregnant
women to continue working as long as their physicians permit. Despite
management assurances regarding job security, several employees
expressed doubts that women would retain full seniority, although they
corroborated the bank's claim that workers returning from leave are
sure to find some job available to them.

Minority Lending

Citizens and Southern's minority lending efforts are part of the
responsibilities of a wholly-owned subsidiary called the Community
Development Corporation. C.D.C. was established in 1968 to implement
the bank's Georgia Plan, a comprehensive attempt to "achieve positive
community goals that will improve the living and working environment."
The president of C.D.C. is William Van Landingham, a Citizens and
Southern executive vice president, and its staff consists of six
people in Atlanta plus approximately 20 more in 10 other Georgia cities.

Citizens and Southern's ultimate minority lending goal is to transform
C.D.C. transactions into regular commercial loans, and it has actually
done so in several cases in which viable businesses have grown from
soft loans. The bank's credit criteria are: (a) management ability,
including the applicant's character and previous experience as an
employee, in the absence of experience as an employer; (b) the ability
to repay the loan; and (c) benefits to the community. Manufacturing
and contracting operations, retail stores, and restaurants are considered
beneficial; pool halls and night clubs are normally considered accept-
able, although the bank did finance one liquor store because the only
other dealer had allegedly been overcharging local residents.

Loans are packaged and serviced by the C.D.C. staff, sometimes supplemented by the bank's own personnel. The work load is heavy: Mills Lane

has said, "You don't make a[soft]loan and turn a man loose"; and in C.D.C.'s Atlanta office, three staff members handle 50-60 businesses. In its response to the American Bankers Association Urban Affairs Survey, Citizens and Southern indicated that management aid to minority business consumes 400 hours per month at an aggregate monthly cost to the bank of $1,800.

C.D.C. was originally capitalized at $1 million; a second million was added in January 1970. In all, $10 million has been committed to the program, but management maintains that no ceiling has been fixed. The number and value of loans has increased each year.

Year	Gross Value	Number of Loans
1970	$1,568,754	228
1969	770,530	113
1968	171,617	12

Loans average about $20,000 apiece, with the great majority going to the retail and service area. Breakdowns of the Georgia Plan, shown below, are the only ones available; the total outstanding is close to $3 million.*

Type of Loan	Number of Loans	Gross Value
Manufacturing	1	$ 18,634
Wholesaling	0	0
Construction	5	111,806
Professional	1	9,317
Services	33	745,377
Retail Trade	2	46,586
Other	1	825,000
	43	$1,786,722

Interest rates are the same as those in conventional lending, but amoritzation schedules are flexible. The debt to equity ratio (the ratio of long-term debt over one year to the net worth of the firm) averages nine to one and up. C.D.C. does some financing of lines of credit and some short-term seasonal financing, but no factoring.

Only 20 loans, representing $142,000 of the $3 million total, have been charged off since C.D.C.'s inception. Delinquencies have also been reasonbaly low, averaging less than 5% of both the number and dollar volume of all soft loans. In its own analysis of the program, C.D.C. has concluded that "negative results point to insufficient performance, either by the customer or by C.D.C.; some deficient areas can be attributed to both parties. In almost every case, failures were a result of simply not following good lending procedures and

---

* (The remaining $1.3 million in soft loans is not broken down by the race of the borrowers.)

judgment." Specifically, the bank found that each unsuccessful loan was marked by at least one of these weaknesses: (1) failure to determine managerial ability beforehand; (2) inadequate character references; (3) failure to require estimates and documentation of plant and equipment costs, administrative expenses and sales; or (4) failure to require some investment by the borrower. (Citizens and Southern profile results, pp.2-3).

Citizens and Southern is the only sample bank which does not use S.B.A. guarantees at all, attributing its policy to the agency's restrictions upon the kind of loans it will guarantee and to excessive red tape. Assistant vice president Richard B. Jones says, "We like to do things and get them done." And Mills B. Lane has stated, "We have never believed that a government guarantee makes a bad loan better. The losses we have taken have been borne by private enterprise and not by the taxpayer."

Mr. Jones believes that C.D.C. would be profitable right now if enough money--perhaps $10 million--were outstanding. He maintains that Citizens and Southern is willing to meet whatever demand for loans exists in the minority community, and Mr. Lane has repeatedly stated that C.D.C.'s capitalization is not fixed, but the bank claims that no further demand exists at present.

Early in 1972, the bank bought $20,000 of stock in Minbank. Management says that Citizens and Southern has worked intimately with two black-owned Georgia banks, Carver State and Citizens Trust, and that the success of the two ventures has reinforced its conviction that direct involvement is more effective than participation in organizations like Minbank, which it considers fragmented.

CONTINENTAL ILLINOIS NATIONAL BANK & TRUST COMPANY
231 South LaSalle Street, Chicago, Illinois 60690 (312/828-2345)

Number of Employees: 8,207
Number of Branches: 1

	1971	1970
Deposits (in billions of dollars as of December 31st):	$8.5	$7.2
Per Share Net Operating Earnings:	$4.11	$3.39

	U.S.A.	City	C.E.P. Sample
1970 Rank by Deposits	8	1	4

President: Tilden Cummings
Chairman: Donald M. Graham
Board of Directors: Robert E. Anderson
James F. Bere
Philip D. Block, Jr.
George R. Cain
Gordon R. Corey
Stewart S. Cort
Lester Crown
Tilden Cummings
Donald M. Graham
William A. Hewitt
William B. Johnson
George E. Keck
Robert H. Malott
Robert L. Milligan
Graham J. Morgan
John H. Perkins
Keith R. Potter
William J. Quinn
Robert W. Reneker
Arthur M. Wood
Joseph S. Wright

Although Continental Bank was slow to produce hard data, it permitted
two and a half days worth of interview time--more than any other
bank; was the only institution to permit observation of its operations
department; and replied to the Council's request for information with
a 47-page narrative. Its cooperation was rated Good.

Employment

All Continental board members, and all executives at or above the vice
presidential level, are white men. One woman and one black man are
second (assistant) vice presidents. Minorities constitute 20.3% of
the entire staff and 4.5% of all officials and managers. Conversely,
2.8% of them are officials and managers, and 88.0% are office and
clerical workers. Women represent 52.5% of the total work force and
13.2% of all officials and managers. The distribution of female
employees is 3.2% official-managerial and 87.0% office-clerical.

See Table 3.

Affirmative Action

Continental initiated its affirmative action program for minorities
in May 1969. The compliance officer is Gene Croisant,
vice president for personnel. He is assisted by second vice president
Robert Ganchiff, to whom two personnel officers and an industrial
psychologist report.

At the time of the C.E.P. interviews, in November 1971, no separate
affirmative action program for women had been written. The bank says
that women are included in its "general affirmative action statement"
and that a personnel department subdivision has been established to
monitor the status of female employees. In support of its claim that
women hold responsible positions throughout the bank, Continental listed
18 women with titles ranging from "operations analyst" at the managerial
level to second vice president in the commercial banking department.
Continental also says:

> We have a committee monitoring issues raised by the women's
> liberation movement....This group keeps abreast of all
> legislative developments pertaining to women's rights,
> familiarizes itself with the objectives of various women's
> organizations, and exchanges information with other banks
> and corporations as a learning experience to help us respond
> more effectively to expectations.

However, when asked for a racial and sexual breakdown of officers
with authority to make loans of various sizes, the bank replied,
"Since the number of minority group and women officers having loan
authorization is obviously limited...we are not providing the tabular
data requested."

Continental says that "the program of expanding promotional opportunities
for women employees has···been pursued aggressively for several years

Table 3

Occupations	Total Minorities	Total Males	Total Females	Total All Employees
Officials and Managers	43	826	126	952
Professionals				
Technicians	69*	835*	169*	1004*
Sales workers				
Office and Clerical	1337	1494	3420	4914
Craftsmen				
Operatives				
Laborers				619 **
Service Workers				
TOTAL	1520	3560	3929	7489

* Figures are for total of Professionals, Technicians and Sales workers.

** Figure includes total of all employees in Blue Collar and Service Worker positions.

and is currently receiving even greater emphasis." Yet a bank brochure called "The Woman's Touch" suggests a different attitude. Its cover shows a pair of female hands arranging roses in a bud vase. Inside, "women who are seeking the stimulation and rewards of a business career but who have not worked in recent years" are offered "a wide variety of opportunities" consisting of six "interesting jobs": receptionist, secretary, typist, customer service representative, proof machine operator, and general clerk. The booklet contains no indication that these jobs are also open to men or that higher-level work may be possible for the woman resuming a career outside the home. The back of the booklet bears the legend "an equal opportunity employer."

Recruiting

A team of ten, including two women and two minority group members, is responsible for college recruiting. Other minority people participate in the process on a part-time basis. Recruitment statistics cannot be analyzed because Continental would not supply the total number of hires for each of the three years nor distinguish between women recruited from predominantly female schools and those hired on coed campuses. In 1971, three offers were made to students on black campuses, but all were turned down.

	TOTAL		BLACK		FEMALE	
	# Colleges	# Hires	# Colleges	# Hires	# Colleges	# Hires
1971	72-74	Data refused	10	0	3	5*
1970	70	Data refused	9	0	3	7*
1969		Data refused	4	0	Data refused	10*

*Includes women recruited from coed campuses

Management appears concerned about its unsuccessful attempts to hire blacks and commented on the matter at length. A bank official indicated that the poor image of Chicago stemming from events associated with the Democratic National Convention of 1968 and the trial of the Chicago Seven, together with the banking industry's generally poor reputation among blacks, have increased the difficulties involved in recruiting minorities.

Testing

Testing is used for placement purposes, only. All tests have been validated for minority groups; nevertheless the vocabulary test has been eliminated.

Training

Continental's executive-management training process is formally called the Administrative Development and Operations Management Program. Unlike comparable procedures at Chase, First Pennsylvania, and Citibank,

Continental's program includes preparation for operations management
as well as for lending, and the number of trainees is therefore
relatively large.

	TOTAL		BLACK		HISPANIC		OTHER		WHITE	
	M	F	M	F	M	F	M	F	M	F
1970	163	38	6	4	3	0	2	0	152	34
1969	133	30	6	3	0	0	2	0	125	27
1968*	13	0	1	0	0	0	0	0	12	0

*Figures for 1968 do not include Operations Management.

In 1970, females constituted 18.9% of the trainees, minority females
2.0%. Minority men and women combined represented 7.5% of the total,
minority males alone 5.5%. The program's importance is underlined
by Continental's statement that "it is only on extremely rare occasions
that the bank hires   directly at the officer level."

First-Time Promotions to Officer

In 1970, females received 3.3% of all promotions to officer status and
minority men 4.4%. The percentage for minority females during 1968-70,
as already noted, was zero.

	TOTAL		BLACK		HISPANIC		OTHER		WHITE	
	M	F	M	F	M	F	M	F	M	F
1970	88	3	3	0	0	0	1	0	84	3
1969	42	1	1	0	0	0	0	0	41	1
1968	67	1	0	0	1	0	1	0	65	1

Continental argues that these figures are misleading because they do
not include holders of operational and technical jobs who supposedly
"have no need" for titles because they do not have personal contact
with customers.

Ratings

Ratings are conducted 90 days after an employee begins work and every
6-12 months thereafter, depending on the level of the job. In November
1971, management stated that employees see and sign their rating
reports, but in August 1972 a personnel department representative
stated that supervisors need only "discuss" them with employees and
that the latter are not required to see and sign them.

Maternity

A pregnant woman may continue working as long as she wishes provided
that she has permission from the bank's physician. Asked why
authorization from her own doctor would not suffice, management replied
that the requirement is necessary to ensure "adequate" medical attention for workers.

Minority Lending

Since its inception in 1968, Continental's minority economic development program, Group 4B, has made 54 loans totaling $3,800,000--
approximately 17 loans a year averaging $73,000 each. Four of the
54 failed. All except eight of the 54 carried Small Business Administration guarantees; the eight represented $150,000, or less than 4% of
the total amount.

Continental maintains that the figures do not show "the great amount
of effort expended": the bank has conducted 495 interviews with
potential borrowers, some of whom were interviewed several times. The
interviews generated 111 loan applications, 57 of which were eventually
rejected.

Group 4B is headed by second vice president Roland Burris, a black
graduate of Howard University Law School who has been with Continental
for seven years. Mr. Burris is enthusiastic about minority lending,
but he expresses some regret that Chicago banks are legally restricted
to the unit system because he believes that these loans could be better
serviced through branch banking. Although Mr. Burris says that "the
best loan is a manufacturing loan," most transactions fall into the
retail and service category. The bank tries to "funnel 'Ma and Pa'
operations back to the community banks" because they are "the toughest
to deal with...They cause more problems and require more time" than
loans of other types, he says.

Asked to explain the bank's involvement in minority economic development in light of the criticism of Andrew Brimmer and others, Mr. Burris
said that Mr. Brimmer ignores the fact that such programs foster an
awareness of the business tradition and a sense of personal pride.
When he visits an entrepreneur's home, Mr. Burris says, he senses that
the children are impressed by the fact that their father has dealings
with a banker.

DETROIT BANK AND TRUST COMPANY
Fort at Washington, Detroit, Michigan 48231 (313/222-3300)

Number of Employees: 2,455
Number of Branches: 51 (Detroit only)

	1971	1970
Deposits (in billions of dollars as of December 31st):	$2.2	$2.0
Per Share Net Operating Earnings:	$6.35	$6.17

	U.S.A.	City	C.E.P. Sample
1970 Rank by Deposits	25	2	10

President: C. Boyd Stockmeyer
Chairman: Raymond T. Perring
Board of Directors: Walter L. Cisler
                     Frank A. Colombo
                     Rodkey Craighead
                     Louis A. Fisher
                     Walter B. Ford, II
                     Edward J. Giblin
                     William E. Grace
                     Leslie H. Green
                     William B. Hall
                     Charles H. Hewitt
                     Jason L. Honigman
                     Roblee B. Martin
                     James McMillan
                     Paul S. Mirabito
                     Raymond T. Peering
                     H. Lynn Pierson
                     Robert F. Roelofs
                     C. Boyd Stockmeyer
                     Arbie O. Thalacker
                     Cleveland Thurber
                     Herbert B. Trix
                     Kenneth J. Whalen
                     James O. Wright
                     William R. Yaw

Detroit Bank and Trust Company was unwilling to cooperate in any way and was therefore rated Poor for participation. In a telephone conversation on July 22, 1970, Detroit Bank and Trust's president, C. Boyd Stockmeyer, indicated that the C.E.P. questionnaire would not be filled out. He cited two reasons for his decision: first, that too much time is being spent on studies rather than on action; and second, that "the questionnaire requests information which the bank does not even release to its stockholders, let alone the general public." When a Council representative visited Detroit in November 1971, he telephoned Mr. Stockmeyer to ask that interviews with bank management be permitted so that some material could be obtained in the absence of statistical information. The C.E.P. representative stressed that the two other Detroit sample banks, which had also withheld hard data, had granted this request. Mr. Stockmeyer again declined, through his secretary.

C.E.P. spoke with several employees, who seemed eager to comment. Due to management's inaccessibility, the accuracy of their information could not be checked. One worker claims that "the worst part about [Detroit Bank and Trust] is that they're smug." A second maintains that "the bank thinks it's doing a lot, but it isn't." Both observers prefer to remain anonymous.

Employment

The board of directors is 100% white male. There are two or three black male officers, one of whom has responsibilities in the trust area, but no female minority officers. Detroit Bank and Trust is the only sample bank in the city with a female full vice president; she is an economist and is the highest-ranking woman at the bank. There are ten other female executives, but only five of them have officer status; the others are branch managers. One female employee says that these women "may have the titles, but they don't really do any decent banking jobs."

Affirmative Action

Data refused.

Recruiting

Data refused.

Testing

Data refused.

Training

Detroit Bank and Trust apparently has no formal executive-management training program. Instead, it has an "administrative training program" which is geared to the branches. Even so, the first female trainee in the bank's history was chosen only recently. Male participants in this program receive official titles within 6-12 months of their entrance into it.

Data refused.

Ratings

Two employees indicate that bank policy does not require that employees see and sign their rating forms.

Maternity

Data refused.

Minority Lending

Data refused.

FIRST NATIONAL BANK OF ATLANTA
2 Peachtree Street, P.O. Box 4148, Atlanta, Georgia 30302 (404/588-5000)

Number of Employees: 2,335
Number of Branches: 22

	1971	1970
Deposits (in millions of dollars as of December 31st):	$791.2	$789.5
Per Share Net Operating Earnings:	$4.55	$4.15

	U.S.A.	City	C.E.P. Sample
1970 Rank by Deposits	80	3	16

President: Edward D. Smith
Chairman: Edward D. Smith
Board of Directors: Ben S. Barnes
                     Henry L. Bowden
                     W. Lee Burge
                     W. Clair Harris
                     Oliver M. Healy
                     Alfred W. Jones
                     Alfred D. Kennedy, Jr.
                     W.L. Lee
                     Lucien E. Oliver
                     Frank E. Owens, Jr.
                     Allen Post
                     E. Edmund Rast
                     J. Leonard Reinsch
                     Roy Richards
                     E. English Robinson
                     Edward D. Smith
                     Robert H. Tharpe
                     Pollard Turman
                     Milton Weinstein
                     Charles R. Yates
                     Church Yearley

First National Bank of Atlanta ia rated Poor because it denied all forms of assistance. C.E.P.'s request for information elicited a letter from Edward D. Smith, chairman, dated September 3, 1971. It is quoted in full:

> The First National Bank of Atlanta will not be able to participate in the Council on Economic Priorities' study of minorities and women in banking. I regret that we cannot meet all requests for participation in research projects, but your study does not meet any of the criteria we have established for screening such requests.
>
> I point out that you would be doing us a disservice--and certainly not reporting objectively or factually--if you attempt to discuss our minority efforts without our input, or if you suggest an "unwillingness to inform the public."

The "criteria we have established for screening" were never identified.

A second request, asking that this position be reconsidered, was addressed to Church Yearley, vice chairman of the bank and regional director of the Urban Affairs Committee of the American Bankers Association. His reply, a letter dated December 10, 1971, is also quoted in its entirety:

> There has been no change in our position regarding your study of minorities and women in the banking industry since Mr. E.D. Smith's letter of September 3.

Later, C.E.P. asked the head of the Urban and Community Affairs Committee, Peter McNeish, whether he saw any inconsistency in Mr. Yearley's serving with the group but not encouraging his own bank to take part in a study of industry practices in areas of social concern. Mr. McNeish answered that Mr. Yearley's attitude on this and related matters was one reason why "I don't want him on my committee" and then went on to criticize Atlanta banks for their minimal participation in Minbank.

The only bits of information available came from a bank source who indicated that, as of February 1972, First National had one female assistant vice president, other women officers at lower levels, and no black officers of either sex.

108

FIRST NATIONAL BANK OF CHICAGO
One First National Plaza, Chicago, Illinois   (312/732-4000)

Number of Employees: 5,758
Number of Branches   1

	1971	1970
Deposits (in billions of dollars as of December 31st):	$7.2	$6.3
Per Share Net Operating Earnings:	$3.42	$3.13

	U.S.A.	City	C.E.P. Sample
1970 Rank by Deposits:	10	2	5

President: John E. Drick
Chairman: Gaylor Freeman
Board of Directors: Thomas G. Ayers
                     Edward F. Blethner
                     Edward D. Carlson
                     Gaylord Donnelley
                     John E. Drick
                     Marshall Field
                     Gaylor Freeman
                     William B. Graham
                     John D. Gray
                     Robert P. Gwinn
                     Ben W. Heinemen
                     Robert S. Ingersoll*
                     Frederick G. Jaicks
                     Brooks McCormick
                     Louis M. Menk
                     Gordon M. Metcalf
                     Lee L. Morgan
                     William Wood Prince
                     Gerald A. Sivage
                     Robert D. Stuart, Jr.
                     John E. Swearingen

* Resigned to become Ambassador to Japan

First National Bank of Chicago supplied copies of its 1971
E.E.O.-1 form and American Bankers Association Urban
Affairs Survey in lieu of the C.E.P. questionnaire, but it
refused to permit interviews with management because it objected to
the cost in time and money. Waid R. Vanderpoel, vice president and
administrative assistant to the chairman of the board, stated in a
letter:

> I do hope you can appreciate our position. Many of us
> feel that the battle for ending job discrimination
> towards minority groups and women is a past fight.
> ....Though I can only give you a personal opinion, I feel
> sure we are doing everything humanly possible to make sure
> that there are no legitimate grounds for criticism. We
> have a rising number of black officers and an increasing
> number of women officers. We have training programs and
> hiring policies all geared to make sure that we are
> observing not only the letter of the law but the spirit
> of cooperation to eradicate any remaining vestiges of
> discrimination.

Mr. Vanderpoel also indicated that the refusal to permit interviews
stemmed partly from the bank's concern about "the well-publicized
example of a somewhat similar survey conducted at a large eastern
bank which involved the expenditure of a great deal of time and
money and led to unhappiness on both sides"--an obvious reference
to Leinsdorf's Citibank. Cooperation was considered Good.

Employment

There are no minority or female members of the board of directors.
The highest ranking blacks (five) are officers, and the highest ranking women are the several female assistant vice presidents. According to the bank's 1971 annual report, no women officers are assigned
to the domestic commercial lending, bond, or corporate securities
areas. The trust department does have three--one of whom is an
assistant vice president in the legal section. There were two female
officers each in personnel and operations, and two in the executive
department, which includes comptrollership and auditing.

Minorities of both sexes account for 21.2% of all employees. 3.6% of
all officials and managers, or 39 people, are minority workers, and
all but eight of the 39 are male. Women constitute 48.3% of the entire
work force and account for 133 or 12.5% of the officials and managers;
all but eight of the 133 are white. 5.2% of all female employees are
officials and managers while 88.8% of all women and 96.8% of minority
women do office and clerical work.

See Table 4.

Affirmative Action.

The bank's affirmative action program for minorities was established in
December of 1970. John Clark, vice president, is the bank's compliance
officer .

Table 4

OCCUPATIONS	MALE EMPLOYEES					FEMALE EMPLOYEES					TOTAL ALL EMPLOYEES
	Total Males	Minority Groups				Total Females	Minority Groups				
		NEGRO	ORIENTAL¹	AMERICAN INDIAN¹	SPANISH AMERICAN¹		NEGRO	ORIENTAL¹	AMERICAN INDIAN¹	SPANISH AMERICAN¹	
OFFICIALS AND MANAGERS	935	18	6	1	6	133	7	1	0	0	1068
PROFESSIONALS	227	3	5	0	6	50	7	1	0	0	277
TECHNICIANS	198	41	3	0	6	29	0	2	0	0	227
SALES WORKERS	117	5	1	0	3	73	6	1	0	0	190
OFFICE AND CLERICAL	1055	152	23	0	32	2273	646	31	2	89	3328
CRAFTSMEN (Skilled)	60	2	0	0	1	0	0	0	0	0	60
OPERATIVES (Semiskilled)	-	-	-	-	-	-	-	-	-	-	-
LABORERS (Unskilled)	7	1	0	0	0	0	0	0	0	0	7
SERVICE WORKERS	138	11	1	0	3	1	0	0	0	0	139
TOTAL	2737	233	39	1	57	2559	666	36	2	89	5296

111

Recruiting

First National recruits at predominantly black and female campuses, although the institutions were not identified.

TOTAL		BLACK		HISPANIC		OTHER	
M	F	M	F	M	F	M	F
167*	81*	5	5	0	0	8	6

*Includes all holders of college degrees hired in 1970.

32.6% of all 1970 college hires were white or minority women; minority women represented 4.4% of the total. Minority men alone accounted for 5.2% of all hires, and minority men and women combined represented 9.7%.

Testing

Testing procedures have been validated for minorities.

Training

Data refused.

First-Time Promotions to Officer

Data refused.

Ratings

A source at the bank told C.E.P. that employees see and sign their rating reports.

Maternity

One employee says that women must begin their maternity leaves at the end of the seventh month of pregnancy, a policy which would violate the Equal Employment Opportunity Commission guidelines if it remains in force. Leaves extend up to three months after the birth of the child.

Minority Lending

Minority business lending is directed by vice president Russell H. Ewert. The bank reported these figures in response to the A.B.A. Urban Affairs questionnaire.

	Gross Value Outstanding	Number Loans (New)
1970	$3,464,673	54 (27 new)
1969	1,350,811	27
1968	no program	no program

From December 31, 1969 to December 31, 1970, the gross amount outstanding rose by more than $2 million, and 27 new loans were made. Average loan size was almost $80,000, the highest in the C.E.P. sample.

At least part of the packaging is developed from opportunities presented by local agencies like the Chicago Economic Development Corporation (C.E.D.C.), the Talent Assistance Program (T.A.P.), and the National Economic Development Association (N.E.D.A.). First National also refers business to $1-million M.E.S.B.I.C.

No further data were obtained because interviews were not permitted.

FIRST NATIONAL CITY BANK
399 Park Avenue, New York, New York 10022 (212/559-1000)

Number of Employees: 37,000 (F.N.C.B. Corp.)
Number of Branches: 200 (Domestic)

	1971	1970
Deposits (in billions of dollars as of December 31st):	$24.3	$21.0
Per Share Net Operating Earnings:	$3.09	$2.59

	U.S.A.	City	C.E.P. Sample
1970 Rank by Deposits:	3	2	2

President: William I. Spencer
Chairman: Walter B. Wriston
Board of Directors: William B. Batten
                    Milo M. Brisco
                    John D. deButts
                    Frederick M. Eaton
                    Dr. Louis K. Eilers
                    Dr. Lawrence Fouraker
                    J. Peter Grace
                    Gordon Grand
                    William P. Gwinn
                    Amory Houghton, Jr.
                    George P. Jenkins
                    Arthur E. Larkin, Jr.
                    C. Peter McColough
                    Charles B. McCoy
                    Gordon M. Metcalf
                    Roger Milliken
                    Roger S. Oelman
                    Edward L. Palmer
                    Charles M. Pigott
                    William M. Rees
                    William I. Spencer
                    Franklin A. Thomas
                    Albert L. Williams
                    Walter B. Wriston

Our organization is a knowledge factory and our prime
resource is our people, the thousands of members of
Citicorp organizations whose skills and energy are the
bulwark of efficient, worldwide services.

--1971 annual report

The top management is committed to at least equal
opportunity.
                    --Robert Feagles, senior vice
                    president for personnel

Citibank's cooperation was Fair. It originally refused to participate
in the study beyond mailing C.E.P. some newspaper clippings and a copy
of a speech by one of its executives. In a letter dated July 30, 1971,
William Spencer, its president, explained that the bank had just taken
part in the Leinsdorf study at a cost of more then 10,000 hours and
about $250,000 and therefore "we do not think we can possibly impose
another such burden on our employees and we doubt very much that we
could justify another such expenditure to our stockholders." C.E.P.
replied that it appreciated the bank's viewpoint and would be pleased
to accept E.E.O.-I forms and a copy of the bank's American Bankers
Association Urban Affairs Survey as substitutes for its own
questionnaire. In October, Mr. Spencer reiterated Citibank's decision
not to cooperate, this time citing the reason that "we solicit minority
information from our employees in confidence and we do not release the
details to anyone but authorized government agencies." C.E.P. continued
to pursue the matter, and in early 1972 the bank finally agreed to
permit two interviews with management and to release information on
minority economic development. It refused statistics on employment
practices, however, although a highly-placed source at the Dreyfus
Corporation says that the bank released such data to Dreyfus' Third
Century Fund*, which owned 8,500 shares of F.N.C.B. Corporation common
stock as of May 31, 1972.

Employment

Franklin Thomas, the black president of the Bedford-Stuyvesant Restoration Corporation, was elected to the Citibank board of directors in
1970. There are no female board members.

F.N.C.B. Corporation, the Citibank holding company, employs 37,000 people
world-wide; 17,000 of them work in New York City. The bank staff
includes approximately 2,000 officials and managers, of whom 35 are
senior vice presidents and another 200-250 vice presidents. All senior
vice presidents are white men. Four of the vice presidents are women--
a greater number than at any other sample bank--including one who
works in the international department, one in corporate banking, and
two in investment management. The highest ranking blacks are at the
assistant vice president level, 9,700 or 57% of the bank's
staff is female; 3,400 or 20% black; and 1,700 or 10% Hispanic American,
several of whom are vice presidents.

* (A mutual fund which invests in corporations on the basis of their
  social, as well as financial, performance.)

For a discussion of the Wadsworth sex discrimination suit against Citibank, see "Women: Legal Challenges."

Affirmative Action

An affirmative action program was established in 1967, and it now applies to women. Mr. Feagles is the compliance officer.

Recruiting

Citibank's extensive campus recruiting is conducted by a seven-member college and professional recruiting team which is headed by a black man, Wilbur Hobbs, and which includes one other black and two women. In 1971, the bank visited 61 colleges and universities, ten of which were largely black. The Wadsworth suit charges that it did not go to any women's schools until 1972; management, however, denies this.

Testing

Data refused.

Training

The College Training Program, a highly structured project combining on-the-job learning with formal, in-bank courses, is a key route to top management positions; Mr. Feagles says that it will "hopefully supply, in the long run, the senior decision-makers of the organization." Roughly 200 people are trained each year. An unofficial source at the bank says that fourteen women have entered the program thus far in 1972, and that eight of them are being prepared for commercial banking, corporate banking, and investment management-- areas historically closed to women and minorities. One of the women is black, and about half hold M.B.A.s.

C.E.P. learned that an employee of the international department, a woman who had earned masters degrees in French and German and has a working knowledge of four languages, spent approximately four years in a job requiring her to update travel cards, among other tasks. Her requests that she be enrolled in the executive training program or transferred to another job were denied. When her boredom and disgust became apparent, she was asked to resign. She inquired what would happen if she refused to do so and was advised by a bank offical that Citibank could "make things pretty difficult" for her if she ever tried to get charge cards at any large New York retail stores.

First-Time Promotions to Officer

Data refused.

Ratings

Bank policy encourages supervisors to show employees their ratings, and several staff members confirmed that the policy is honored. However, a woman who resigned from the bank in the summer of 1971 stated that she never saw or signed her report during her four years of employment, and Beverly Wadsworth informed C.E.P. that she was instructed to initial a blank rating sheet which was then filled in secretly by her supervisor.

Maternity

At the time of the C.E.P. interviews, pregnant women who wanted to work past the fifth month had to obtain a physician's authorization once a month after that date. Leaves extend for six months from the date of childbirth and are granted in cases of adoption, too.

Minority Lending

Citibank's minority lending program was reorganized and formally initiated in July of 1971, three years later than those at the other New York sample banks. The program operates under First National City Capital Corporation, a small business investment company (S.B.I.C.) which is a wholly-owned subsidiary of F.N.C.B. Corporation. (S.B.I.C.s and M.E.S.B.I.C.s are described under "Blacks: Minority Lending.")

According to William G. Herbster, senior vice president in charge of Citibank's urban affairs department, F.N.C. Capital Corporation has eight or nine lending and investment officers, each of whose portfolios includes minority or soft loans. This manner of distribution is used because "with one guy exclusively on soft loans, he's going to lose perspective, get frustrated," said Mr. Herbster.

As of December 31, 1971, F.N.C. Capital had made 36 soft loans and investments averaging $63,200 each, and totaling in excess of $2 million. Approximately 49% of the dollar value was guaranteed by the S.B.A. or some other agency.

Citibank maintains that these figures do not truly reflect the extent of its involvement. It provides technical assistance to minority economic development organizations like the Bedford-Stuyvesant Restoration Corporation. Furthermore, Mr. Herbster says, 15 to 25 Citibank branches are located in "low-income and/or minority-intensive areas," and many of the loans which they grant must be going to minority businesses. While his assertion may be accurate, it gives no clue as to whether such loans are soft, for lending to minority business is not necessarily lending to borrowers who do not meet conventional credit standards.

FIRST PENNSYLVANIA BANKING AND TRUST COMPANY

15th and Chestnut Streets, Philadelphia, Penn. 19102 (215/786-5000)

Number of Employees: 6,525
Number of Branches: 77

	1971	1970
Deposits (in billions of dollars as of December 31st):	$2.9	$2.0
Per Share Net Operating Earnings:	$2.77	$2.46

	U.S.A.	City	C.E.P. Sample
1970 Rank by Deposits:	20	1	7

President: James F. Bodine
Chairman: John R. Bunting
Board of Directors: Gustave G. Amsterdam
James F. Bodine
John R. Bunting
Gerard V. Carey
Joan Ganz Cooney
William P. Davis, III
William L. Day
William P. Drake
Anthony G. Felix, Jr.
Harry J. Gangloff
Robert F. Gilkeson
David H. Harshaw
G. Joseph Keady
Edward T. Moyneham
Henry G. Parks, Jr.
M. Robert Ritchie, Jr.
A. Addison Roberts
Charles R. Tyson
William B. Walker
Philip Zinman

118

The corporation that does not use the power that profitability provides to enter the social arena will become a declining force in our society.

--John Bunting, chairman
1971 annual report

First Pennsylvania Banking and Trust Company released employment and lending data and granted a day for interviews and was therefore judged Good for cooperation.

Employment

First Pennsylvania's board of directors includes the female president of the Children's Television Workshop, Joan Ganz Cooney, a black man, Henry Parks, and a white graduate student, Harry J. Gangloff, all three of whom were elected in 1971. One black man, Elmer Young, Jr., is a full vice president.

Blacks account for 12.6% of the bank's entire work force, and all minorities account for 13.4%. The lion's share of them are found at the office and clerical level (83.6%) or below it (9.0%). Most of the 7.4% of the minority employees who hold upper-echelon jobs are male; 3.9% of all officials and managers are minorities. Women form the majority of the work force, 59.6%. 97.0% of all women and 98.0% of minority females are in office and clerical jobs. Only 1.4% of all female employees are officials and managers, and 6.2% of all officials and managers are female. All but one of the 38 women executives are white.

See Table 5.

Affirmative Action

First Pennsylvania's affirmative action program was adopted in 1967 and affects minorities, only. In March 1972, management stated that a similar plan for women was "near completion." Rudolph Weber, vice president and compliance officer, reports to the head of personnel, senior vice president Walter Powell.

Recruiting

There are three full-time recruiters, all male. One is a minority group member. The bank visits black colleges in the vicinity of Philadelphia and went to a women's campus for the first time in 1972. According to the placement bureau of that school, Beaver College, First Pennsylvania sent a white male who interviewed 10 students without making any job offers. Shortly afterward, he wrote to the college to say that he could not "express an interest in any of the students."

119

Table 5

OCCUPATIONS	MALE EMPLOYEES					FEMALE EMPLOYEES					TOTAL ALL EMPLOYEES
	Total Males	Minority Groups				Total Females	Minority Groups				
		NEGRO	ORIENTAL¹	AMERICAN INDIAN¹	SPANISH AMERICAN¹		NEGRO	ORIENTAL¹	AMERICAN INDIAN¹	SPANISH AMERICAN¹	
OFFICIALS AND MANAGERS	596	20	3	0	1	38	1	0	0	0	634
PROFESSIONALS	112	3	0	0	2	18	1	0	0	0	130
TECHNICIANS	158	14	0	0	0	15	0	0	0	0	173
SALES WORKERS	–	–	–	–	–	–	–	–	–	–	–
OFFICE AND CLERICAL	819	113	1	0	5	2639	367	5	0	21	3458
CRAFTSMEN (Skilled)	–	–	–	–	–	–	–	–	–	–	–
OPERATIVES (Semiskilled)	11	0	0	0	0	1	0	0	0	0	12
LABORERS (Unskilled)	–	–	–	–	–	–	–	–	–	–	–
SERVICE WORKERS	146	49	0	0	0	9	5	0	0	1	155
TOTAL	1842	199	4	0	8	2720	374	5	0	22	4562

	TOTAL # Colleges	TOTAL # Hires	BLACK # Colleges	BLACK # Hires	FEMALE # Colleges	FEMALE # Hires
1971	22	4	5	3	0	0
1970	26	12	5	0	0	0
1969	28	7	2	1	0	0

According to Mr. Powell, the number of graduates hired directly from the campus is small because Philadelphia salary levels are approximately 20% below those in New York.

Unlike many New York and Chicago banks, First Pennsylvania recruits M.B.A.s at only one business school, the Wharton School of Finance. Starting salaries for M.B.A.s are $10-12,000 and may not be competitive with those in the other two cities or in industries other than banking. In addition, First Pennsylvania prefers having its own staff members return to school to earn the degree, rather than hiring M.B.A.s.

Testing

Bank officials say they are re-examining the entire subject of testing and that all such procedures may be discontinued. Management believes that arithmetic-literacy examinations, for example, are valuable, but a great many minority applicants continue to fail them even though they have been validated.

As of March 1972, other tests were "in the process" of being validated. Test scores are no longer supplied to supervisors.

Training

First Pennsylvania has four formal training programs for college graduates which last about two years and lead to: branch management; audit programs; trust and investment; and commercial staff services. The last of these programs, called Credit Workshops, prepares employees to be loan officers. Programs are conducted within the bank by staff members, occasionally supplemented by outside instructors.

Women constituted 11% of all trainees in 1970 , 17% in 1969, and 12% in 1968. In those same years, blacks represented 13%, 6%, and 10%, respectively. Only one black woman was included during that period, and no member of any other minority group took part at all.

	TOTAL M	TOTAL F	BLACK M	BLACK F	HISPANIC M	HISPANIC F	OTHER M	OTHER F	WHITE M	WHITE F
1970	40	5	5	1	0	0	0	0	35	4
1969	54	11	4	0	0	0	0	0	50	11
1968	45	6	4	1	0	0	0	0	41	5

Management estimates that 30-35 of the 60-65 college hires projected for 1972 will be trained for branch management, 17 for audit programs, four for trust and investment, four to six for commercial staff services, and the rest for other types of responsibilities. First Pennsylvania says it would like to see blacks represent about 10-12% of all executive-management trainees and that "realistically speaking" the percentage of females will be under 10%.

First-Time Promotions to Officer

Of 93 employees promoted to officer for the first time during 1968-70, three or 3.2% were white women. None were minorities of either sex.

	TOTAL		BLACK		HISPANIC		OTHER		WHITE	
	M	F	M	F	M	F	M	F	M	F
1970	22	2	0	0	0	0	0	0	22	2
1969	28	1	0	0	0	0	0	0	28	1
1968	40	2	0	0	0	0	0	0	40	2

Management indicated that five blacks advanced to the officer level in 1971 but did not supply information for other minority groups or for women for that same year.

Ratings

Every worker's performance is appraised, and each department has its own rating system. The bank encourages supervisors to show ratings to employees. It hopes to have employees see and sign their reports by 1974; First Pennsylvania is leaving that much lead time so that supervisors can be "sensitized" to the "problems of minorities and women" before the new policy takes effect.

Maternity

Women were required to leave work at the end of the seventh month of pregnancy and to inform the bank of their intention to return within 90 days after giving birth. After that notification, they were permitted 90 days' additional leave. Management admitted that the policy would probably need revision in light of the Equal Employment Opportunity Commission findings in other industries.

Minority Lending

First Pennsylvania's minority lending program, the Economic Development Unit (E.D.U.), began in 1966. It is headed by Elmer Young, Jr., who was brought into the bank a year ago as its first, and to date only, black full vice president. Like the rest of management, he emphasizes First Pennsylvania's sense of "corporate commitment." Mr. Young himself is not a lending officer. A lending officer does report to him, as do two men who follow loans in two parts of Philadelphia.

E.D.U. is less centralized than similar programs at Chase and Citizens and Southern. All loans originate at branches and are packaged by outside agencies such as the Office of Minority Business Enterprise, Wharton, and E.A.S.E. (a division of Temple University). E.D.U. has no separate budget; instead, each branch manager is given discretion up to the limit of her or his lending authority, and loans of any kind beyond that ceiling are routed up through the hierarchy for approval. Applications cannot be rejected by branches without Mr. Young's permission.

Available data are scanty, but it is known that First Pennsylvania has made approximately $8 million in loans since 1966, $800,000 of it in 1971 and all except 5-10% of it S.B.A.-guaranteed. About 350 loans are currently outstanding, averaging $35-$40,000 each, although one for as much as $350,000 was recently made. Most soft loans are in the retail area, and refinancing is arranged in about 25% of the cases. The bank will back a failing loan--i.e. charge it off against the reserve for bad loans and provide refinancing under a new note--if the branch manager who made it can prove that everything possible was done to save it. Net losses on S.B.A. loans are averaging about 7%, far below the pre-1966 level of 23%; during those earlier years, First Pennsylvania worked with a consortium of lending institutions in the city.

The bank also participates in a new Philadelphia M.E.S.B.I.C. capitalized at $750,000, with an additional $250,000 available for administration overhead. First Pennsylvania itself contributed $64,250.

GIRARD BANK
One Girard Plaza, Philadelphia, Penn. 19101 (215/585-2000)

Number of Employees: 3,245
Number of Branches: 70

	1971	1970
Deposits (in billions of dollars as of December 31st):	$2.3	$2.1
Per Share Net Operating Earnings:	$6.28	$6.27

	U.S.A.	City	C.E.P. Sample
1970 Rank by Deposits:	23	2	8

President: William B. Eagleson, Jr.
Chairman: Stephen S. Gardner
Board of Directors: Geoffrey S. Smith
                     Graeme Lorimer
                     Morris Duane
                     John R. Park
                     George H. Brown, Jr.
                     E.H. Smoker
                     George R. Clark
                     Robert M. Wachof
                     Russell N. Ward
                     William J. Young
                     Stephen S. Gardner
                     Eric A. Walker
                     Courtlandt S. Gross
                     E. Markoe Rivinus
                     Randall E. Copeland
                     Henry M. Chance, II
                     John T. Gurash
                     William B. Eagleson, Jr.
                     Lewis H. Van Dusen, Jr.
                     Isadore M. Scott
                     Leon H. Sullivan
                     Howard O. Beaver, Jr.

The cooperation of Girard Bank is judged Fair. William B. Eagleson, its president, responded to the first inquiry with "general information which I think will be responsive to your detailed request":

> ...The bank has consistently endeavored to go beyond requirements in our efforts to recognize the importance of providing minority groups with employment and better economic opportunity.
>
> Some of our employees with over forty years of service recall that when they were first employed Girard had black staff members. About twenty-five years ago the bank began a program to increase the number of black employees in what is generally termed clerical work. The number of minority group members has steadily risen. They presently constitute approximately 17% of our total staff and include representation in our supervisory, administrative and officer staffs. This figure is much higher than the percentage of non-whites in the population of the seven counties in southeastern Pennsylvania in which we are permitted to have banking offices....Girard's "affirmative action" policy is a well established practice and is recognized in our community....
> ....
>
> Many supervisory and administrative positions are occupied by women and...the number of women officers is increasing. The bank has had a maternity leave policy for many years.
>
> ...We have a unit of two officers and an administrator who serve as the focal point for making loans and providing guidance to minority group businessmen. These specialists are available to our officers and branch managers and furnish the kind of advice and assistance that can develop and make bankable loans that might otherwise be considered not creditworthy. They also directly provide advice and information. We have invested substantial amounts, with other Philadelphia banks, in programs for making loans to small businesses which, to a large extent, are owned by minority group members.
>
> This general summary of our activities in the areas in which you specified interest represents, I believe, both the practice of equal opportunity employment and a demonstration of social concern.

Upon receipt of these statements, C.E.P. wrote to Mr. Eagleson requesting substantiation of them. None was forthcoming. Repeated attempts to obtain specific material through the office of the Reverend Leon Sullivan, founder and president of Opportunity Industrialization Centers, Inc. (O.I.C.) and Girard's only black director, also met with failure. A man who identified himself as one of Reverend Sullivan's assistants suggested that the bank might cooperate in exchange for information about the other two Philadelphia sample banks.

125

The suggestion was rejected because C.E.P. policy prohibits release of information about a corporation prior to the release of the full study to the general public.

The bank did permit an interview with John P. Adams, an executive vice president. At its outset, Mr. Adams said that Girard has an "obligation to·do something with the Federal government" but recognizes no such obligation toward "self-appointed" private outside organizations like C.E.P. The interviewer therefore invited him to answer those parts of the questionnaire with which he felt more comfortable. Mr. Adams responded, "You mean the questionnaire you sent the bank? How long are you going to be here?!"

Mr. Adams' role appeared to be largely ceremonial, despite executive trappings like a secretary, a large, wood-paneled office with adjoining conference room, and a private bathroom. He did not know, for instance, that the A.B.A.'s Urban and Community Affairs Committee had recently visited Girard to encourage increased minority employment and lending. Nor did he appear to know what an affirmative action program is. And when asked if the bank's entry-level employment tests had been validated, Mr. Adams said, "Oh, sure, we're been using these tests since the '50s."

Employment

From Girard and other sources, C.E.P. learned that the bank employs about 3,200 people, roughly 17% of whom are black. Girard claims that it has approximately a dozen black officers, including a recently-hired administrative vice president; however a staff member who requested anonymity insists that there are no more than four. There are 20 female officers; the highest-ranking of these is a senior investment officer, a status equivalent to a vice presidency; but she does not have account responsibilities, and her job is restricted to research.

More employees and former employees expressed dissatisfaction with Girard than with any other sample bank. A black man, formerly an assistant branch manager, characterizes Girard as "very, very pre-judiced." In support of his contention, he says that he single-handedly brought in $750,000 worth of new business in a campaign involving nearly 4,000 people yet was later refused a $10/week raise. He left Girard for another bank which offered him an annual salary increase of $3,000. Another black employee complained of receiving a phone call from a secretary on the bank's staff asking whether two employees who had been invited to attend an intramural banquet were black; she wanted to know so that all black guests could be seated at the same table.

Affirmative Action

Girard has an affirmative action plan for minorities but had none for women at the time of the interview.

126

Recruiting

Girard recruits at three black colleges. Mr. Adams identified two of them as Lincoln University and Virginia Union and tentatively identified the third as Delaware State. Mr. Eagleson says that the bank supplies "employment information" to two women's colleges, but he does not name them nor explain whether anything more than the mailing of an occasional pamphlet is involved. Management says the recruiting team includes minorities and women but declines to give supporting figures.

Testing

Data refused.

Training

Data refused.

First-Time Promotions to Officer

Data refused.

Ratings

Employees are rated annually. They are said to discuss the subject with supervisors but neither see nor sign the reports.

Maternity

As noted above, Girard "has had a maternity leave policy for many years."

Minority Lending

Data refused.

MANUFACTURERS HANOVER TRUST COMPANY
350 Park Avenue, New York, New York 10022 (212/350-3300).

Number of Employees: 12,793
Number of Branches: 155

	1971	1970
Deposits (in billions of dollars as of December 31st):	$12.2	$11.1
Per Share Net Operating Earnings:	$2.86	$2.77

	U.S.A.	City	C.E.P. Sample
1970 Rank by Deposits:	4	3	3

President: John F. McGillicuddy
Chairman: Gabriel Hauge
Board of Directors: William O. Beers
                     William S. Beinecke
                     Viscount De L'Isle
                     James D. Finley
                     Robert V. Hansberger
                     Gabriel Hauge
                     Henry H. Henley, Jr.
                     John E. Heyke, Jr.
                     Barron Hilton
                     William F. Laporte
                     William L. Lindholm
                     John F. McGillicuddy
                     R.E. McNeill, Jr.
                     George B. Munroe
                     Richard S. Reynolds, Jr.
                     Robert W. Sarnoff
                     Walter F. Thomas
                     Lynn A. Townsend
                     Nathan H. Wentworth
                     F. Perry Wilson
                     David G.Yunich
                     George G. Zipf

After some initial hesitation, and several meetings with Council
on Economic Priorities representatives, Manufacturers Hanover Trust
agreed to provide employment and lending data and to submit to
interviews. Its cooperation was judged Good.

Employment

There are no women or minority group members on the board of directors.
The roster of full vice presidents includes one woman and one Hispanic
American male, and a black male is an assistant vice president. All
minority females in the officials and managers category hold super-
visory positions which do not carry officer status. Management claims
that racial and sexual identification of officers with lending authority
is "not available."

The distribution of official and managerial jobs at Manufacturers
Hanover is better than that of any other reporting bank: 13.4% of
these positions are held by white women, 3.4% by minority women, and
9.9% by minority men.

Women make up 55.7% of the total work force. 9.9% of them are in
executive positions and 86.8% in office and clerical jobs. 3.4%
of all minority women are executives and 95.7% of them are in the
office and clerical category. 9.9% of minority males are executives,
68.9% in office and clerical.

See Table 6.

Affirmative Action

Manufacturers Hanover adopted its affirmative action program in 1969.
Management states that the original version of the plan "encompasses
sex discrimination." Senior vice president Frederick W. Oswald has
charge of personnel and acts as the compliance officer.

Recruiting

A staff of four, including two minority people and one woman, comprise
the college recruiting team. About four of the 25-30 schools visited
each year have been black: Hampton Institute in Virginia, Virginia
State, Morgan State in Maryland, and--when competition with other
companies permits--Howard University in Washington. The bank did
not recruit on predominantly female campuses during 1969-71, and it
cancelled an appointment to visit Connecticut College this year.

	TOTAL		BLACK		FEMALE	
	# Colleges	# Hires	# Colleges	# Hires	# Colleges	# Hires
1971	29	12	4	5	0	0
1970	24	8	3	0	0	0
1969	31	8	4	5	0	0

Table 6

OCCUPATIONS	MALE EMPLOYEES					FEMALE EMPLOYEES					TOTAL ALL EMPLOYEES
	Total Males	Minority Groups				Total Females	Minority Groups				
		NEGRO	ORIENTAL[1]	AMERICAN INDIAN[1]	SPANISH AMERICAN[1]		NEGRO	ORIENTAL[1]	AMERICAN INDIAN[1]	SPANISH AMERICAN[1]	
OFFICIALS AND MANAGERS	2147	61	5	3	51	709	50	3	3	28	2856
PROFESSIONALS	285	12	4	0	13	130	7	0	0	2	415
TECHNICIANS	327	61	4	0	29	71	11	0	0	1	398
SALES WORKERS	–	–	–	–	–	–	–	–	–	–	–
OFFICE AND CLERICAL	2454	531	26	3	278	6204	1646	59	16	662	8658
CRAFTSMEN (Skilled)	25	0	0	0	0	0	0	0	0	0	25
OPERATIVES (Semiskilled)	60	11	0	0	6	0	0	0	0	0	60
LABORERS (Unskilled)	–	–	–	–	–	–	–	–	–	–	–
SERVICE WORKERS	391	76	1	2	38	31	3	0	0	0	422
TOTAL	5689	752	40	8	415	7145	1717	62	19	693	12834

No females were hired from women's campuses during 1969-71, but over a third of all college hires in those years were black.

Testing

As of early 1972, employment tests were "in the process" of being validated for minority groups. The bank has agreed to participate with Columbia University in a five-year, Federally-funded program meant "to analyze the basic components of skill and aptitude for entry jobs."

Training

Sixty per cent of the participants in Manufacturers Hanover's executive-management training program are college recruits; the rest are people who were already employed by the bank. Compared with the five other banks who supplied data for 1970, Manufacturers Hanover ranks at or near the top for inclusion of minority males, minority females, and all females.

	TOTAL		BLACK		HISPANIC		OTHER		WHITE	
	M	F	M	F	M	F	M	F	M	F
1970	*272	29	25	4	8	0	1	1	238	24
1969	*302	22	20	1	1	1	1	1	280	19
1968	*279	21	24	0	4	0	0	0	251	21

* At year-end.

Of 301 participants during 1970, 34 or 11.3% were minority men, 24 or 8.0% were white women, and five or 1.7% were minority women.

First-Time Promotions to Officer

In 1970, 8.7% of first-time promotions to officer went to white women, and nine promotions accounting for 4.9% went to minority men. No minority women were similarly upgraded in any of the years.

	TOTAL		BLACK		HISPANIC		OTHER		WHITE	
	M	F	M	F	M	F	M	F	M	F
1970	168	16	4	0	5	0	0	0	159	16
1969	117	14	3	0	1	0	1*	0	112	14
1968	137	33	3	0	2	0	0	0	132	33

*Oriental

Ratings

Bank employees are rated at least once a year. They are shown the report and asked to sign it. A female officer states that the four-page rating report for officers is longer than that for lower-echelon staff members and that executives are not shown the last page, which comments on their potential.

Completed ratings are key-punched into a computer. Print-outs then rate performance on a scale of one through five, rate potential on a scale of A through D, and show the length of time the worker has spent in one job. Management believes this procedure helps identify skills and increases upward mobility for all personnel.

Maternity

A woman may continue working past her sixth month of pregnancy if her personal physician submits written authorization at the end of each month after that. Leave extends up to six months from the date of departure and is then renewable.

Minority Lending

The minority loan program began in 1968 and is headed by Gus McCarthy, a vice president. The bank declined to provide much concrete information because "[we] do not have figures for specific types of loans."

At the time of the interview, the bank's minority portfolio consisted of 89 loans. Thirty-two of these carried Small Business Administration guarantees and were not broken down into industry type. Of the remainder, 29 were service and retail, nine were construction, six manufacturing, two real estate, and three personal. The dollar value of each category was:

Service/Retail	Construction	Manufacturing	Real Estate	Personal
$973,000/$89,000	$306,000	$507,000	$554,000	$18,000

At its high point, the program had $2,228,000 outstanding. The bank was "exposed" for $1,311,000 of that amount; the rest was guaranteed, mainly by the S.B.A. Another $168,000 was loaned to the Puerto Rican Forum, a local community economic development organization.

MANUFACTURERS NATIONAL BANK OF DETROIT
151 West Fort Street, Detroit, Michigan 48231 (313/222-4000)

Number of Employees: 2,491
Number of Branches: 69

	1971	1970
Deposits (in billions of dollars as of December 31st):	$2.2	$1.9
Per Share Net Operating Earnings:	$6.84	$6.33

	U.S.A.	City	C.E.P. Sample
1970 Rank by Deposits:	27	3	11

President: Dean E. Richardson
Chairman: Roland A. Mewhort
Board of Directors: Louis G. Allen
                      Wendell W. Anderson, Jr.
                      Albert J. Berdis
                      H. Glenn Bixby
                      E. Paul Casey
                      LeRoy W. Dahlberg
                      Max M. Fisher
                      Sherman J. FitzSimons, Jr.
                      William Clay Ford
                      Mervyn G. Gaskin
                      Pierre V. Heftler
                      George M. Holley, Jr.
                      Harry J. Loynd
                      Wilfred D. MacDonnell
                      Wilber H. Mack
                      William A. Mayberry
                      William G. Meese
                      Roland A. Mewhort
                      Donald R. Mitchell
                      William T. Patrick, Jr.
                      Dean E. Richardson
                      Robert P. Scherer, Jr.

Manufacturers National, the youngest Detroit sample bank, was founded in 1933 with Ford money. It began penetrating the retail market during the 1950s, and the bulk of its branch expansion has occurred in the past seven years.

Cooperation is classified as Fair. Manufacturers National Bank granted two days of interviews but released little substantive data. John Ryan, vice president for personnel, says:

> In the banking industry we are very visible. We are approached by many individual people requesting infor-mation, and rather than make judgments about individual groups we have a blanket policy of refusing all requests. There is a strong tendency to look at numbers only and play a numbers game only. I do feel that it is not in the best interest of the bank to release this information. Person-ally, I am particularly proud of what the banks are doing in Detroit.

The first question Mr. Ryan was asked during the interview was "When was the bank's affirmative action program adopted?" After a long pause, he replied that the interviewer was taking out some of his "frustration" upon Mr. Ryan.

The bank's black director, William Patrick, who was elected in 1971, attempted to persuade management to cooperate more fully, but his efforts were unsuccessful.

Employment

Manufacturers National has about 270 officers, including "several" black men and one black woman. No minorities or women are full vice presidents. Six white women are officers: one, who entered that category in June 1971, is in corporate trust; a second is a loan officer in the national division; and a third and fourth are branch managers. Two more are second vice presidents who have spent more than 20 years with Manufacturers National: one is in personnel, and the other has charge of a branch. Women therefore represent 2.2% of all officers.

Manufacturers National would not supply comparable data for minority group members. Although no questions regarding religious minorities were asked, the bank volunteered the information that seven or eight officers are Jewish.

Affirmative Action

Mr. Ryan would not say when the affirmative action program for minorities was established. Nor would he state whether a separate program for women exists. He has since indicated that such a program now exists.

Recruiting

The bank declined to supply data on the composition of its recruiting team. Mr. Ryan stated that Manufacturers National does recruit at black campuses and claims that four men were hired there during 1971. Asked about predominantly female colleges, he responded, "There are no female colleges. They have all gone coed."

Testing

Management would not say whether testing procedures have been validated for minority group members. It says that the bank has not used "cut off" scores in hiring for several years.

Training

Manufacturers National indicates that it "has no formal executive-management training program."

Yet it does have a credit program which feeds personnel to all areas. Employees admitted to it must have a degree in finance or accounting. About a third of the trainees are M.B.A.s, although the bank feels the degree possesses "no great magic."

The bank also has a branch training program for college graduates, which M.B.A.s do not enter because holders of advanced degrees cannot successfully be recruited for this level. The program takes three to five years with the first three months spent working as a teller. Participants are said to include approximately ten blacks.

The total number of trainees in each program and their races and sexes could not be ascertained.

First-Time Promotions to Officer

Of the six females who have achieved officer status, one received her promotion in 1967, three in 1969, and two in 1971. The bank withheld additional data.

Ratings

All employees see and sign their rating reports. If a staff member's rating is below average, a re-evaluation is conducted in 90 days, and the employee again sees and signs the report. No one may be fired without a re-evaluation. When a worker leaves the bank, an exit interview is conducted, usually by the person who originally interviewed her or him; the employee is asked to fill out a questionnaire which solicits comments about the bank, its supervision, and the particular job.

Maternity

As of November 1971, women were required to begin their maternity leaves at the end of the sixth month of pregnancy and were permitted six months' leave after childbirth. This policy has since been changed to comply with new E.E.O.C. maternity guidelines.

Minority Lending

Manufacturers National started its loan program in 1968. It is headed by a vice president in the metropolitan division, Thaddeus J. Winiarski. No figures on the number of loans were released, but an indication of the portfolio's size can be gleaned from the size of the staff, which consists of one full-time person and "two others who allocate about one half of their time each."

Most loans are covered by the Small Business Administration. The rest are relatively small and the bank did not want to spend time coping with the agency's paperwork in order to obtain guarantees for them. Mr. Winiarski says that "the biggest part of financing is in the service and retail area" and that very few loans are in manufacturing, although some construction loans have been made.

Mr. Winiarski's view of minority economic development is less than sanguine: "I think we're flying in the face of a basic problem," he says. "The chances of success are very remote." He foresees little possibility of the bank's making money on the program: "I see problems in breaking even. It takes more time to make a $10,000 loan to a minority business than a $1 million loan to Detroit Edison." He added that loss ratios are difficult to determine because "we spend more time in servicing the account....Instead of a straight $10,000 loss, we experience a $10,000 loss associated with servicing." However, Mr. Winiarski does say that "we're trying to develop a heritage among minority businessmen. Even the failures have a purpose...."

NATIONAL BANK OF DETROIT
Woodward at Fort Street, Detroit, Michigan 48232 (313/225-1000)

Number of Employees: 5,822
Number of Branches: 105

	1971	1970
Deposits (in billions of dollars as of December 31st):	$4.7	$4.0
Per Share Net Operating Earnings:	$6.19	$6.07

	U.S.A.	City	C.E.P. Sample
1970 Rank by Deposits:	16	1	6

President: Charles T. Fisher, III
Chairman: Robert M. Surdam
Board of Directors: A.H. Aymond
                     Henry T. Bodman
                     Ivor Bryn
                     Harry B. Cunningham
                     William M. Day
                     Leland I. Duan
                     Charles T. Fisher, III
                     A.P. Fontaine
                     John B. Ford
                     John F. Gordon
                     Joseph L. Hudson, Jr.
                     Ralph T. McElvenny
                     Dan T. McKone
                     Ellis B. Merry
                     F.W. Misch
                     Peter J. Monaghan
                     George F. Parker, Jr.
                     Robert B. Sample
                     Nate S. Shapero
                     Austin Smith, M.D.
                     George A. Stinson
                     Peter W. Stroh
                     Robert B. Surdam
                     Donald F. Valley
                     Norman B. Weston

In many respects, we are all Equal Opportunity Officers at
National Bank of Detroit. Each of us has a responsibility,
a personal commitment to further the objectives of equality.

> --John H. Lowe, assistant vice
> president and equal opportunity
> officer, quoted in "Equal Oppor-
> tunity at National Bank of Detroit,"
> a booklet, August 1971

Like other banks in the same city, National Bank of Detroit was originally
established with automotive industry money--specifically, with funds
from General Motors--and was wholesale-oriented until it recently began
moving into the retail sector.

Its cooperation was Fair. Like Manufacturers National, National Bank
granted two days of interviews but refused to produce hard data on
employment of minorities and women or on minority lending. In response
to C.E.P.'s first inquiry, Norman B. Weston, then executive vice president, requested more information on the Council and its work. He later
stated that the questionnaire was being filled out but that he was not
sure whether the bank would return it to C.E.P. At length the questionnaire was completed--two Council representatives saw it on an official's
desk during an interview--but the bank refused to release it. William
Blevins, vice president for personnel, explained this decision by saying
that "when you publish raw data it can be misinterpreted. It would be
liable for misinterpretation." The bank's compliance officer, John H.
Lowe, told C.E.P. that he opposed cooperation because the questionnaire
was "too good" and therefore made him "suspicious." A black male
employee of National Bank warned C.E.P. to "remember that this bank is
conservative, very conservative."

Employment

National Bank has no women or minorities on its board of directors.
Aubrey Lee, a vice president who heads the minority lending program,
is the highest-ranking black and the only black vice president at any
Detroit sample bank. Management says that there are "several" additional black male officers at lower levels but offers no details. The
National Bank staff of 5,200 is 65% female, but there are no women vice
presidents or assistant vice presidents and, according to one source,
"none are scheduled." The highest-ranking women are assistant cashiers.
A female employee maintains that only four white women are officers;
that the first of the four did not receive that designation until
1969; and that the other three were so designated in the last year
or two after one of them had spent more than 25 years on the staff.
Management claims that "many" supervisors are women. No minority
women hold officer status, and no women work in commercial lending.

Affirmative Action

Mr. Lowe is the compliance officer, as noted above. He reports to
Mr. Blevins. National Bank's affirmative action program was established
in 1965. During the C.E.P. interview in November 1971, Mr. Lowe

indicated that he was working on a separate program for women and commented that "it will be a real problem." He did not explain why.

Recruiting

According to Mr. Lowe, who also has charge of recruiting, National Bank visits six black campuses but no predominantly female colleges. One recruiter is black; management stated that there are women on the team but would not say how many.

National Bank prefers that college graduates have backgrounds in finance, accounting, or general business, and it emphasizes the M.B.A. when hiring people for commercial lending. Recruitment statistics were withheld.

Testing

Data refused.

Training

National Bank has six training programs for college hires; commercial lending, trust administration, investment research, computer systems, branch management, and comptrollership. Training for credit areas like commercial lending lasts 18-24 months. At the time of the interview, National Bank was "working on its second black trainee" and had "just recently hired one woman in the trust investment program."

First-Time Promotions to Officer

One woman was promoted to assistant cashier in 1969 and now works in the trust area. She was the first woman in the bank's history to attain management status and the first to become an officer. All other information was refused.

Ratings

Employees are rated annually, but management considers it unnecessary for them to see or sign their reports because supervisors undergo one day of sensitivity training and because supervisors discuss the reports with the employee. Exit interviews are conducted for employees who are fired or who resign, and several months later a questionnaire is sent to the former staff member asking the reason for the departure and soliciting comments on the bank's management.

Maternity

Women are expected to begin their maternity leaves at the end of the sixth month. Management characterizes this policy as "flexible" but does not elaborate. If unaltered, it would violate the 1972 Equal Employment Opportunity Commission guidelines. Leaves extend up to three months after childbirth.

Minority Lending

The minority lending program, initiated in February of 1969, is headed by Aubrey Lee, as noted above. He is assisted by four lending officers, two credit analysts, and a secretary. Mr. Lee reports to Joseph Conway, the senior vice president who has charge of National Bank's metropolitan division. Mr. Conway summarized the status of the program by commenting, "...We have the money. There's absolutely no shortage of money.... There is a shortage of qualified personnel to document and make loans."

What Mr. Lee labels "watch" loans originate at the branches and are usually less than $100,000 apiece. Roughly half of all proposals are turned down, and the rejected applications are reviewed by a committee. Packaging, which is handled by the main office rather than by outside agencies, takes about one month. Servicing consumes approximately 50% of Mr. Lee's own time. If an entrepreneur needs outside professional services, like those of an accountant, the bank will help arrange them and will try to obtain favorable fees for the entrepreneur. Although Mr. Lee considers it difficult to reverse a downward trend once a business seems destined to fail, National Bank does much refinancing nonetheless.

In Mr. Conway's judgment, the basic problem inherent in the encouragement of minority enterprise is that black consumers are more interested in a business' prices than in its owner's race. National Bank has found that its best results come from loans made to blacks who have been in business for at least two years. According to Mr. Lee, these people have "respect for the buck. The chances of such a person's 'making it' are tremendous." When asked whether loans of this nature are genuinely "soft," Mr. Lee responded affirmatively: "These guys are the ones who are barely staying alive." National Bank is reluctant to grant "Ma and Pa" loans, as it has in the past, considering them "artificial" because operations on so small a scale do not create jobs.

Management acknowledges that Detroit banks are more reliant on Small Business Administration guarantees than are banks in other cities and that its own use of them is very heavy. It claims that it can obtain S.B.A. approval within two or three weeks' time. National Bank has also made soft loans that may or not need the agency's guarantee "for obvious reasons--to better our record for successful loans ."

The bank was unwilling to supply any statistical data.

NATIONAL BANK OF WASHINGTON
619 14th Street, N.W., Washington, D.C. 20005 (202/624-3000)

Number of Employees: 773
Number of Branches: 19

	1971	1970
Deposits (in millions of dollars as of December 31st):	$388.8	$458.3
Per Share Net Operating Earnings:	$2.56	$4.84

	U.S.A.	City	C.E.P. Sample
1970 Rank by Deposits:	144	3	18

President: True Davis
Chairman: True Davis
Board of Directors: Honorable True Davis
                     Edward C. Baltz
                     Crosby N. Boyd
                     A. Britton Browne
                     D. Randall Buckingham
                     Edward L. Carey
                     Liz Carpenter
                     Harry L. Curtis
                     Joseph B. Danzansky
                     Frank E. Fitzsimmons
                     Lepold V. Freudberg
                     William S. Harps, M.A.I.
                     Webb C. Hayes, III
                     Eliot Janeway
                     W. Ledru Koontz
                     Honorable Marjorie McKenzie Lawson
                     Robert C. Mayer
                     H. Gabriel Murphy
                     Elwood R. Quesada
                     Benjamin T. Rome
                     Honorable George A. Smathers
                     Bruce G. Sundlun
                     Dr. J. Lawn Thompson, Jr.
                     John J. Wilson
                     William C. Yowell, Jr.

141

National of Washington is the smallest sample bank, ranking 144th in the United States by 1970 deposits.

The bank is notable for its close associations with labor unions and former government officials. More than half of its stock is owned by the United Mine Workers, and The National Bank of Washington recently suffered a severe deposit loss when Federal courts ordered the union to withdraw $85 million in pension funds. In a separate matter, U.M.W. president, W.A. "Tony" Boyle, resigned from the bank's Board of Directors. Mr. Boyle had been one of three U.M.W.-affiliated directors listed in the 1970 annual report; last year's report lists only one, the union's general counsel, Edward L. Carey.

National Bank's president and board chairman is True Davis, an ambassador to Switzerland during the Johnson Administration.

A black board member, Patricia Roberts Harris, was ambassador to Luxemburg under the Kennedy Administration and chaired the credentials committee of the 1972 Democratic National Convention.* Among the other board members are George Smathers, former senator from Florida, and Frank E. Fitzsimmons, who succeeded James R. Hoffa as president of the International Brotherhood of Teamsters. Clark Clifford, who was Secretary of Defense under Lyndon Johnson, formerly sat on the board, as well.

National's cooperation was judged Good. Although E. Gordon Owens, senior vice president, maintains that the bank "has nothing to hide," the first request for information was refused and the bank did not agree to participate until the Council had pursued the matter.

Employment

One Hispanic American male, but no women of any race, is a full vice president. A black man, Emmett Rice, became a senior vice president in 1972, and two white women are assistant vice presidents. Women and minorities respectively account for 10.1% and 2.5% of the officials and managers. 57.3% of the entire work force is female, and 94.8% of these employees are located in office and clerical jobs; another 2.7% are executives. 86% of the minority women do office and clerical work; 14% are found below that level, none above it. Almost half the minority males--45.5%--perform clerical jobs, while 2.7% hold executive positions. The percentage of these men in blue collar and service jobs, 51.8%, is the highest at any of the six banks reporting.

See Table 7.

---

*(She resigned from the board, and was elected to that of Chase Manhattan, in 1972.)

Table 7

OCCUPATIONS	MALE EMPLOYEES					FEMALE EMPLOYEES					TOTAL ALL EMPLOYEES
	Total Males	Minority Groups				Total Females	Minority Groups				
		NEGRO	ORIENTAL	AMERICAN INDIAN	SPANISH AMERICAN		NEGRO	ORIENTAL	AMERICAN INDIAN	SPANISH AMERICAN	
OFFICIALS AND MANAGERS	107	2	0	0	1	12	0	0	0	0	119
PROFESSIONALS	-	-	-	-	-	-	-	-	-	-	-
TECHNICIANS	-	-	-	-	-	-	-	-	-	-	-
SALES WORKERS	-	-	-	-	-	-	-	-	-	-	-
OFFICE AND CLERICAL	159	43	2	0	5	420	51	6	0	10	579
CRAFTSMEN (Skilled)	-	-	-	-	-	-	-	-	-	-	-
OPERATIVES (Semiskilled)	-	-	-	-	-	-	-	-	-	-	-
LABORERS (Unskilled)	-	-	-	-	-	-	-	-	-	-	-
SERVICE WORKERS	64	57	0	0	0	11	11	0	0	0	75
TOTAL	330	102	2	0	6	443	62	6	0	10	773

143

Lending Authority

No females or minority group members are authorized to make unsecured loans in excess of $5,000 and secured loans in excess of $30,000 without permission from a supervisor.

Affirmative Action

Mr. Owens is the compliance officer. National's affirmative action program was established in May 1969. Asked whether a separate program for women exists, the bank answered, "No. All employees are treated equally." Management says it has no program intended to deal with issues raised by the women's liberation movement.

Recruiting

National does no college recruiting.

Testing

All testing was discontinued on February 1, 1972.

Training

National has had a small executive-management training program since 1970. In its first year, it comprised 12 trainees. Three of them or 25% were black men, one or 8.3% was a white woman, and none were minority females.

	TOTAL M	TOTAL F	BLACK M	BLACK F	HISPANIC M	HISPANIC F	OTHER M	OTHER F	WHITE M	WHITE F
1971	9	2	3	2	0	0	0	0	6	0
1970	11	1	3	0	0	0	0	0	8	1
1969					no program					
1968					no program					

Last year, there were 11 trainees, nearly half of whom were black or white women or black men.

First-Time Promotions to Officer

Six white women were promoted to officer for the first time in 1970, thereby receiving 12.5% of all such promotions. Two minority males, who represented 4.2% of all recipients, also achieved that status, but no minority women did so in any of the three years.

144

	TOTAL		BLACK		HISPANIC		OTHER		WHITE	
	M	F	M	F	M	F	M	F	M	F
1970	42	6	2	0	0	0	0	0	40	6
1969	12	2	0	0	0	0	0	0	12	2
1968	11	3	0	0	0	0	0	0	11	3

Ratings

Mr. Owens states that National Bank uses a rating system and that employees see and sign the reports.

Maternity

Pregnant women may continue work for as long as their doctors permit. Leaves extend for six months after childbirth.

Minority Lending

National Bank has no lending program specifically designed for minority business. However, it was planning such a program at the time of the interview, subject to the availability of one of its black employees to head it.

The bank made 16 regular commercial loans totaling $720,000 to minority businesses. Another four amounting to $320,000 were pending disbursement, and five more for $545,000 were awaiting S.B.A. approval. A National Bank officer states that the bank will consider loans which are credited through the S.B.A.

National Bank is one of several District of Columbia banks to participate in a M.E.S.B.I.C. capitalized at $168,000.

145

NORTHERN TRUST COMPANY
50 South LaSalle Street, Chicago, Illinois 60690 (312/346-5000)

Number of Employees: 2,424
Number of Branches: 1

	1971	1970
Deposits (in billions of dollars as of December 31st):	$2.0	$1.7
Per Share Net Operating Earnings:	$6.97	$7.49

	U.S.A.	City	C.E.P. Sample
1970 Rank by Deposits:	30	3	12

President: Douglas R. Fuller
Chairman: Edward Byron Smith
Board of Directors: John A. Barr
                     Karl D. Bays
                     Silas S. Cathcart
                     Albert B. Dick, III
                     Douglas R. Fuller
                     Charles W. Lake; Jr.
                     Donald B. Louries
                     Thomas G. Murdough
                     John S. Reed
                     Leo H. Schoenhofen
                     Gilbert H. Scribner, Jr.
                     Edward Byron Smith
                     Harold Byron. Smith
                     Omer G. Voss
                     J. Harris Ward

146

Northern Trust was very reluctant to participate. Management eventually consented to an interview and was therefore given a cooperation rating of Fair, but it staunchly refused to impart much substantive data; employment statistics were particularly skimpy.

The bank's essentially conservative nature is suggested by the fact that all male employees were required to wear hats en route to and from work until a few years ago.

Employment

As of the end of 1971, Northern Trust's staff of 2,363 included 360 minority workers or 15.3%. The bank had 360 <u>officers</u>, of whom 17 or 4.7% were women, and two or three of these women were said to be located in commercial banking. During 1970, women accounted for 3.6% of all officers, and three minority group members--a black, a Hispanic American, and an Oriental--accounted for an additional 0.8%.

After the study's project directors, one woman and one man, had visited Northern Trust, the bank sent C.E.P. a letter whose salutation read "Gentlemen." It stated, "We feel there is no reason for not considering a woman for any position or official post in the bank" and went on to say that

> in 1966 we employed six women as officers or .021% of our official staff. In 1972 we have 17 women officers or .047% of our official staff. The letter was in error. The actual percentages were 2.1% and 4.7%. Although we are far from satisfied, we believe that our progress since 1966 in the employment of women officers is improving as our percentage of women officers more than doubled, although the total official staff increased only about 24%.

Affirmative Action

The affirmative action program was adopted in July of 1969. In February 1972, James L. Porter, senior vice president for personnel, wrote that "this program applies, of course, for women...."

Recruiting

Mr. Porter heads the recruiting team; management was uncertain whether it consists of five or six people. Northern Trust expects to visit some 25 colleges and universities in 1972, including Ivy League schools, Stanford, and Duke. It also plans to continue seeking talent at predominantly black schools like the Atlanta complex, Morehouse, and Central States.

In 1970, 12 offers were made to black college graduates; six hires resulted. Last year, three offers were made and two accepted. Management acknowledges that its success in recruiting blacks has been limited owing to a "considerable resistance to living conditions in the Chicago area" and to the conservative reputation of banking in general, and

147

Northern Trust in particular, among blacks.

Data on recruitment of college women were refused.

Testing

Management states that employment tests "are relatively few and have been validated."

Training

Data refused.

First-Time Promotions to Officer

Northern Trust would not discuss first-time promotions to officer. It did state that employees who hold an M.B.A. commonly become officers within two to three years, while those with baccalaureate degrees need an additional year's training before reaching that status.

Ratings

Employees are rated at least once a year. There are two types of ratings, one for performance and one for development; the latter applies to staff members in the top nine of the bank's 18 grades. The present policy, under which workers see and sign their reports, may be revised because of "problems inherent" in it stemming from the expanding size of the work force, Mr. Porter says.

Maternity

Women are expected to start their maternity leaves at the end of the seventh month but may continue beyond that date with a physicians's approval. Leave extends for three to four months after childbirth.

Minority Lending

Northern Trust initiated its minority lending program in 1968 as part of the metropolitan division, which is responsible for commercial lending for Chicago.* It has a three-member staff: two people work full-time, and the third is a trainee on temporary assignment.

An estimated 25-30 loans totaling $1.3 to $1.5 million have been made. At the end of 1971, 21 loans totaling $700,000 were outstanding. (This figure was supplied during the interview; in a subsequent letter, the bank quoted a figure of $630,000.), with an additional $300,000 committed. Loans average $35-$40,000 and are concentrated in the retail area. About half the businesses obtaining them are start-ups, i.e. new operations; the remainder are buy-outs, i.e. existing enterprises being sold by the previous owners. Most packaging is handled by outside agencies like

---

*(As opposed to national and international lending.)

Chicago Economic Development Corporation and National Economic Development Association.

Assistant cashier Michael Smith, who has charge of the program, indicates that the demand for soft loans is small; in his words, "Nobody is fighting for the loans we have." Northern Trust relies "heavily" on S.B.A. guarantees but refuses to release any figures to C.E.P. Management claims that the few non-S.B.A. loans constitute the majority of all bad loans in the program.

As an alternative to refinancing, the bank prefers to increase the maturity, rather than the monthly payment schedule, of a bad loan. All transactions to date have been term loans which mature (I.e. must be repaid in full) in two and a half to ten years. They usually carry a moratorium on principal which may last up to a year in the case of start-up businesses. Interest rates rarely exceed 2% over prime and can be renegotiated as the prime rate fluctuates.

Northern Trust says it has a "commitment to invest in a Chicago M.E.S.B.I.C." but would not elaborate.

PHILADELPHIA NATIONAL BANK

Number of Employees: 3,070
Number of Branches: 59

	1971	1970
Deposits (in billions of dollars as of December 31st):	$2.2	$2.0
Per Share Net Operating Earnings:	$4.38	$3.90

	U.S.A.	City	C.E.P. Sample
1970 Rank by Deposits:	24	3	9

President: G. Morris Dorrance, Jr.
Chairman: G. Morris Dorrance, Jr.
Board of Directors: Peter A. Benoliel
                     Herbert W. Blades
                     John P. Bracken
                     T.A. Bradshaw
                     Paul J. Cupp·
                     G. Morris Dorrance, Jr.
                     James L. Everett, III
                     F.O. Haas
                     Samuel J. Korman
                     John McDowell
                     G. Willing Pepper
                     Frederic A. Potts
                     Robert H. Potts
                     Roy G. Rincliffe
                     G. Stockton Strawbridge
                     F. K. Tarbox
                     E. R. Telling

150

The cooperation of Philadelphia National Bank was Fair. It refused to make employment and lending data available, saying that it has had to get "hard-nosed" because it has been flooded with such requests and dislikes playing a "numbers game." "Even the Italians" have requested data, said Tom Palmer, senior vice president in charge of personnel; "We have an Italian mayor. I don't know what more the Italians want," he added.

In a letter dated August 20, 1971, assistant personnel officer Robert A. Evans wrote:

I feel certain that [your]...study will enhance our know-ledge and sensitivity to the minority hiring and promotion policies within the banking industry, and at the same time isolate areas which need improvement. As for the Philadelphia National Bank, we will not be participating. It has been our practice to share this type of minority statistical infor-mation only with the Federal Government (Department of Trea-sury) and its affiliated agencies. We do appreciate the invitation, and wish you and your staff the very best in this endeavor.

Employment

Philadelphia National employs approximately 3,070 people. C.E.P. estimates that 522 or 17% of them are black. Bank sources say that three blacks are officers and that all of them are assistant cashiers, the lowest-ranking job in the officer category. Thirteen of the 370 officers listed in the bank's annual report have recognizably female names; the highest is an assistant vice president. During 1971-72, Philadelphia National hired three people at the officer level--Mr. Palmer and two others; Mr. Palmer was "not sure" if either of the others was black.

Affirmative Action

The bank says it has an affirmative action program for minorities and is in the process of developing one for women.

Recruiting

Philadelphia National says it recruits at several black colleges, including Howard, Lincoln, and Wilberforce Universities, Hampton Institute, Virginia Union, and Morgan State. There is no recruiting team as such. The only permanent recruiter is Mr. Evans, who is black. When other staff members are needed, they are borrowed from the personnel department and from line positions throughout the bank, with black and female officers said to be among those chosen for the purpose.

Testing

The bank says that entry-level tests are in the process of being validated.

Training

Data refused.

First-Time Promotions to Officer

Data refused.

Ratings

Staff members are appraised annually by their supervisors but neither see nor sign the reports. Supervisors are supposed to discuss them with employees, but Mr. Palmer admits that there is no guarantee that the procedure is actually followed.

Maternity

A maternity leave can begin at any time during pregnancy and continue for six months after the child is born.

Minority Lending

The minority lending program is headed by Wilson DeWald, a former Ph.D. candidate in history who is still in his twenties. He joined the Philadelphia National staff three years ago and became interested in minority lending while he was a credit trainee.

He withheld most of the statistical data requested, but a bank publication says that the minority loan portfolio was valued at $939,999 in 1971, up $515,000 from 1970. During this year, the publication states, delinquencies dropped from 24% to 9.0% of the loans outstanding. The average loan is $25-$30,000; the largest was $110-$120,000.

Mr. DeWald says that most transactions carry Small Business Administration guarantees and come under the retail heading. No manufacturing loans are made, primarily because few people apply for them and because "capital for manufacturing is so enormous and the structuring so complex that no one has figured out a way of doing it on straight debt" when the prospective entrepreneur has little or no equity. (I.e. savings or other financial resources with which to start the business.) Most loans go to buy-outs, which the bank prefers because the existence of an established clientele ensures that "there is cash flow from day one." Potential borrowers usually have a minimum of five years' experience in the same type of enterprise, and they must have an accountant before and after the transaction occurs. They must also have access to a lawyer, but need not have one on retainer.

The bank maintains contact with minority clients by telephone and by personal visits every four weeks or so--more frequently with "new and shaky" businesses. Mr. DeWald remarks that managerial assistance involves a lot of work outside office hours, but regards his efforts as an expression of his commitment to the inner city.

RIGGS NATIONAL BANK
1503 Pennsylvania Avenue, N.W., Washington, D.C. 20013 (202/624-2000)

Number of Employees: 2,041
Number of Branches: 17

	1971	1970
Deposits (in millions of dollars as of December 31st):	$941.8	$884.3
Per Share Net Operating Earnings:	$9.31	$8.15

	U.S.A.	City	C.E.P. Sample
1970 Rank by Deposits:	68	1	14

President: John M. Christie
Chairman: L.A. Jennings
Board of Directors: William O. Bant
                    Charles A. Camalier, Jr.
                    Karl J. Corby
                    Lorimer A. Davidson
                    Floyd E. Davis, Jr.
                    R. Roy Dunn
                    Milton L. Elsberg
                    James E. Fitzgerald
                    Charles C. Glover, III
                    Thomas M. Goodfellow
                    Melvin Bell Grosvenor
                    Randall H. Hagner, Jr.
                    Edward K. Jones
                    W. John Kenney
                    J. Willars Marriott
                    James B. Morrison
                    Richard A. Norris
                    Andrew Parker
                    Ralph A. Pfeiffer, Jr.
                    Robert H. Smith
                    Samual Spencer
                    Curtis S. Stevart
                    John W. Thompson, Jr.
                    George O. Vass, Jr.

153

Riggs National was unwilling to participate in any way and was therefore rated Poor. In a letter dated August 2, 1971, John M. Christie, president, explained that "because of the ever-increasing number of questionnaires received in recent years, our bank formulated a policy of answering only those questionnaires received from governmental and quasigovernmental organizations which regulate national banks." He went on to say that Riggs had just completed an "exhaustive" questionnaire from the Department of Housing and Urban Development. C.E.P. telephoned Mr. Christie from New York and again while its representatives were in Washington. None of the calls was returned.

A bank source indicates that Riggs appointed its first and only black officer in April 1970, but that the officer later resigned so that all officers were white as of March 1972. A high-level Treasury official confirms this information and states that Riggs' minority staff constitutes about 38% of all employees. Asked whether Riggs is making any special effort to enlarge the number of black officers, the bank source replied, "Riggs doesn't make any special effort for anything." Three assistant cashiers are female. There are no women in commercial lending.

TRUST COMPANY OF GEORGIA
Pryor Street & Edgewood Avenue, Atlanta, Georgia 30302 (404/588-7711)

Number of Employees: 2,256
Number of Branches: 20

	1971	1970
Deposits (in millions of dollars as of December 31st):	$946.0	$825.7
Per Share Net Operating Earnings:	$4.93	$4.49

	U.S.A.	City	C.E.P. Sample
1970 Rank by Deposits:	75	2	15

President: Augustus H. Stern
Chairman: George S. Craft
Board of Directors: Jack Adair
J. Paul Austin
C.H. Candler, Jr.
James V. Carmichael
J.M. Cheatham
R. Howard Dobbs, Jr.
Charles H. Dolson
Charles W. Duncan, Jr.
Wadley R. Glenn, M.D.
John D. Goodloe
John W. Grant, Jr.
Sartain Lanier
Wilton Looney
Arthur L. Montgomery
William A. Parker
W.A. Pulver
Richard H. Rich
O. Wayne Rollins
James M. Sibley
William P. Simmons
Hughes Spalding, Jr.
William C. Wordlaw

155

Trust Company of Georgia provided no cooperation whatsoever and was therefore termed Poor. The bank sent no written reply to C.E.P.'s correspondence. A Council representative made a follow-up visit to group vice president James Ray while in Atlanta in February 1972. On that occasion, Mr. Ray said that Trust Company had made "a group decision" not to participate because it operates only in the metropolitan Atlanta area, is concerned with its immediate community, and therefore sees little reason for involving itself in a study whose scope is national. He added that C.E.P. would be notified by mail if this ruling were changed upon reconsideration. No further word was received.

A bank source indicates that Trust Company of Georgia has ten white female officers, all below the level of vice president. Women are reportedly expected to begin their maternity leaves at the end of the fifth month of pregnancy.

Findings

The Council on Economic Priorities has found:

---that employment discrimination against minorities and women is endemic to commercial banking;

---that a majority of the commercial banks studied are unwilling to permit public scrutiny of their employment and minority lending practices; and

---that both the secrecy and the discrimination are perpetuated by Federal law, policy and complacency.

More specifically, the C.E.P. has ascertained the following:

1. Minorities: In five of the six cities studied, minorities constitute a smaller proportion of the workers in the three-bank aggregates than in the city work force as a whole. Only in New York are minorities employed at a higher level. The cities with proportionally the smallest representation of minority group members in the banks are Atlanta (where minorities account for 50% of the city labor force but only 14% of the workers at the three top banks) and Washington (70% of the city, 33% at the top banks.)

Minority bank employees are restricted primarily to office and clerical jobs and to blue collar and service positions. Office and clerical workers are primarily women; blue collar workers are largely males. The percentage of blue collar and service workers who are minority group members ranges from a low of 14% in Chicago to a high of 90% in Atlanta. Minority workers comprise a low of 15% of office and clerical workers in Atlanta and a high of 42% in New York. Although 25% of the sample banks' employees are minorities, they hold very few (only 9%) professional, technician or sales jobs, and even fewer (6%) official and managerial positions at the 18-bank sample. Most of those who do are minority men. Minorities constitute a maximum of 8% of all official-managerial staff members in New York and a minimum of under 1% in Atlanta.

2. Women: In all six cities studied, women are employed in percentages exceeding their share of the city labor force.

Women are, however, heavily concentrated in low-level, poorly-paid positions where the outlook for advancement is bleak. Nearly 73% of the office and clerical jobs in the sample are held by women. Likewise, in the three-bank aggregates, they comprise from 67% of all such employees in Chicago to 88% in Detroit. Relatively few women hold positions either below or above that level. Only 22% of all professionals, technicians

and sales workers, and only 15% of all officials and managers in the
sample are women, and these women are mostly white. At the three-bank
aggregates, the percentages of professionals, technicians and salesworkers who are women ranges from a low of 16% in Philadelphia to a
high of 40% in Atlanta. Women's share of the executive level is lower;
only 4% of all executive jobs in Philadelphia are held by women, while
in Detroit they comprise a maximum of 19% of all officials and managers.

3. Probability: The probability that an employee of a given race and
sex will be found in a particular job category follows:

PROBABILITY OF EMPLOYMENT IN VARIOUS CATEGORIES
BY RACE AND SEX
18 Sample Banks*

OFFICIALS AND MANAGERS:

White Males	Minority Males	White Females	Minority Females
1/3	1/12	1/17	1/48

PROFESSIONALS, TECHNICIANS & SALESWORKERS:

White Males	Minority Males	White Females	Minority Females
1/5	1/13	1/18	1/67

OFFICE AND CLERICAL:

Minority Females	White Females	Minority Males	White Males
1/1	1/1	1/1	1/3

BLUE COLLAR AND SERVICE WORKERS:

Minority Males	White Males	White Females	Minority Females
1/8	1/16	1/67	1/77

* Listed in ascending order by the small percentage differences
which exist. To obtain these probabilites, which are based upon
E.E.O.C. data for the 18 sample banks, C.E.P. divided the percentage
of a particular group of workers located in a particular job category
into 1.0, then rounded off to the nearest whole number. For example,
2.05% of the black women employed by sample banks are officials and
managers, and .0205 divided into 1.0 equals 48; therefore, the
probability that a worker of that race and sex will be found in that
job category is one in 48.

4. Correlation*:   There is no significant correlation between female and minority employment statistics and (a) the size of an individual bank; (b) percentages of women and minorities in the city labor force; or (c) percentages of women and minorities in the city population.

5. Performance of Individual Reporting Banks   In general, existing patterns for the three-bank aggregates also apply to the individual reporting banks. Minorities, both male and female, are concentrated in office and clerical jobs and in blue collar and service worker positions-- minorities hold from 9% at First National of Chicago to a staggering 91% of blue collar and service jobs at the National Bank of Washington. Likewise, they account for relatively few of the upper-echelon jobs at the banks and the few who do are largely male. Minorities comprise only 7% of all professionals, technicians and sales workers at First Pennsylvania and Continental Illinois; the maximum is 18% at Manufacturers Hanover. At the top of the hierarchy, minority representation is smallest of all, ranging from a tiny 1.4% of all officials and managers at Citizens & Southern to 7% at Manufacturers Hanover. Overall, the two New York banks, Manufacturers Hanover and Chase, have the best records with regard to minorities, hiring them at levels commensurate with their representation in the work force, and placing them in executive positions in greater proportions than any other reporting banks. Citizens & Southern and National Bank of Washington have the poorest records, hiring minorities as levels well below their representation in city work forces, and having the smallest minority representation in executive positions.

Women do not fare significantly better. They constitute approximately 70% of all office and clerical workers at all reporting banks; however, they are not represented in professional, technician and sales or official and managerial jobs in similarly large numbers. Around 20% of professional, technician and sales worker jobs are filled by women at all of the reporting banks except First Pennsylvania (11%). However, only at Manufacturers Hanover do women comprise over 20% of all executives. At First Pennsylvania, in contrast, these women fill only 6% of the official and managerial positions at the bank. Generally, all of the reporting banks hire women in numbers exceeding their share of the city labor forces. For executive positions, however, Manufacturers Hanover has the best record (25% of its officials and managers are females) while First Pennsylvania has the worst (6%).

6. Cooperation, Resistance, and Their Implications: This is the first C.E.P. project to encounter massive resistance from a majority of the corporations being studied. The uncooperativeness of most sample banks was the key obstacle to C.E.P.'s efforts to evaluate their practices.

---

* At the seven reporting banks, the linear correlation coefficient for female employment and bank size is -.12; that for minority employment and bank size is .24. In three-bank aggregate data, the coefficient for female employment and women in the city labor force is .28; that for black employment and blacks in the city labor force is .49. In three-bank aggregate data, the coefficient for female employment and women in the city population is -.08; that for black employment and blacks in the city population is .29.

In making inquiries, C.E.P. presented the credentials of a responsible research organization. Furthermore, it offered to accept either of two forms which the banks had already completed for other purposes in lieu of its own questionnaire. Nonetheless, only seven banks provided a resonable amount of data; six provided partial data; and five declined to provide any. Cooperation ratings for each bank follow : Very Good: Chase Manhattan, Citizens and Southern. Good: Continental Illinois, First National of Chicago, First Pennsylvania, Manufacturers Hanover, National of Washington. Fair: First National City, Girard, Manufacturers National of Detroit, National of Detroit, Northern Trust, Philadelphia National. Poor: American Security and Trust, Detroit Bank and Trust, First National of Atlanta, Riggs, Trust Company of Georgia.

Inherent in the uncooperativeness are grave implications regarding institutions which enjoy power without accountability. Bank officials issue unsubstantiated generalizations about the importance of social responsibility. But information on their employment and lending practices is virtually unobtainable from any source except the bank itself : the 1964 Civil Right Act prohibits disclosure of such information without the bank's permission and S.B.A. policy contains a similar prohibition for minority lending data. Thus banks make decisions affecting millions of citizens without being subject to the checks and balances of informed public opinion. This secretiveness, coupled with power and protected by law, can increase public cynicism and aggravate social ills.

7.) Changing the Status Quo: No substantial improvement in the proportion of women and minorities in high-level jobs can result if the industry's present programs continue. The percentages of all first-time promotions to officer which went to white women in 1970 ran from the high of 12.5% at National of Washington to the low of zero at First Pennsylvania. Percentages for minority men ranged from 4.9% at Manufacturers Hanover to 1.5% at Citizens and Southern. No minority females were similarly upgraded by any bank which supplied data.

At most sample banks, the composition of executive-management training programs belies official statements about redressing employment inequities. White women constitute a maximum of 17% of all trainees at Continental Illinois and a minimum of 4.0% at Citizens and Southern. The maximum for minority men is 25% at National of Washington--but "25%" means only men; the minimum is less than 4.0% at Citizens and Southern. Minority women fare worst, representing 2.0% of all trainees at Continental Illinois and zero at Citizens and Southern.

The distribution of minority and female executives excludes them almost completely from commercial lending, the most prestigious and best-paid aspect of commercial banking and the commonest route to the top rungs on the executive ladder.

Industry associations' efforts to change the status quo are negligible. Neither the American Bankers Association, the National Bankers Association, nor the National Association of Bank Women has any publicly-stated postion in regard to employment of women. Likewise, the N.B.A. seems unable to take any substantive action in regard to the employment of minorities because of its weak economic status; despite the dynamic leadership of its executive director, Robert Davis, it cannot be

considered a major force for monitoring and increasing black employment
in white banks, particularly at the official-managerial level. The
American Bankers Association has established various minority employment
programs, but the number of participants in them is small. And the
A.B.A.'s Urban Affairs Survey suggests public relations rather than
serious research, for it preserves banks' anonymity.

8.) The Role of Government: Existing laws regarding fair employment are
adequate, but enforcement by the Treasury Department is not. The department has never denied Federal funds to any major bank for non-compliance,
although C.E.P. found extensive and unmistakable employment bias at many
such institutions. The department's attitude appears complacent; it
did not review the world's largest bank until after private citizens had
sued it for alleged sexism. Treasury, the chief enforcement agency for
commercial banking, does not publish the names of banks reviewed, does
not publish the results of reviews, and claims that it keeps no records
of banks which fail to comply because "there just aren't that many."
Hence, the public cannot judge whether the compliance section is allocat-
ing its limited resources wisely and cannot know which banks are obeying
the law and which are flouting it.

9.) Minority Lending: According to data supplied by the Small Business
Administration, the three banks in the six cities studied devote less
than 0.1% of their total assets to minority loans covered by S.B.A.
programs. Only 10 of the 18 banks participate in M.E.S.B.I.C.s. Only
four of the 10--Chase Manhattan, Manufacturers Hanover, Northern Trust
and Continental Illinois--are involved in a M.E.S.B.I.C. capitalized at
or above $1 million, the minimum needed for success, according to two
Harvard Business School professors. Evidence obtained was insuffucient
to permit comprehensive evaluation of individual bank's minority
ecomomic development activities: the banks often refused to supply data,
and a number of them made the novel claim that they themselves were not
sure what they were doing in that area.

Appendixes

Appendix 1

DISTRIBUTION OF JOBS--ABSOLUTE NUMBERS

A. 18 Sample Banks

Race or Sex	Blue Collar & Service Worker	Office & Clerical	Professional, Technical & Sales	Official & Manager
White Male	1,712	9,988	5,216	10,814
White Female	440	25,402	1,636	1,619
Minority Male	807	4,373	481	500
Minority Female	203	12,880	202	288
TOTAL	3,162	52,643	7,535	13,298

B. Three-Bank Aggregates

City	Blue Collar & Service Worker	Office & Clerical	Professional, Technical & Sales	Official & Manager
Atlanta	192	2,485	419	784
Chicago	787	9,691	1,538	2,376
Detroit	463	6,278	841	1,608
New York	1,146	27,836	4,126	7,286
Philadelphia	387	4,145	443	730
Washington	187	2,208	168	514

C. Individual Reporting Banks

Bank	Blue Collar & Service Worker	Office & Clerical	Professional, Technical & Sales	Official & Manager
Citizens & Southern	149	2,082	80	296
Continental Illinois	619	4,914	1,004	952
First National of Chicago	206	3,328	694	1,068
Chase Manhattan	508	14,915	2,442	3,117
Manufacturers Hanover	507	8,658	813	2,856
First Pennsylvania	167	3,458	303	634
National Bank of Washington	75	579	--	119

Appendix 2

DISTRIBUTION OF JOB HOLDERS--ABSOLUTE NUMBERS

A. 18 Sample Banks

Total	White Male	White Female	Minority Male	Minority Female
76,638	27,730	29,174	6,161	13,572

B. Three-Bank Aggregates

City	Total	White Male	White Female	Minority Male	Minority Female
Atlanta	3,880	1,479	1,860	177	364
Chicago	14,392	6,265	5,507	805	1,815
Detroit	9,190	2,793	4,664	402	1,331
New York	40,394	14,214	13,336	4,081	8,763
Philadelphia	5,705	2,085	2,651	325	644
Washington	3,077	894	1,156	371	656

C. Individual Reporting Banks

Bank	Total	White Male	White Female	Minority Male	Minority Female
Citizens & Southern	2,607	889	1,266	134	318
Continental Illinois	7,489	-------Data Refused-----------------			
First National of Chicago	5,296	2,408	1,765	330	793
Chase Manhattan	20,982	7,330	7,315	2,214	4,123
Manufacturers Hanover	12,834	4,474	4,654	1,215	2,491
First Pennsylvania	4,562	1,631	2,319	211	401
National Bank of Washington	773	220	365	110	78

Appendix 3

DISTRIBUTION OF JOB HOLDERS: PERCENTAGES

A. 18 Sample Banks

Employees as Percentage of all Workers		Percentage Employed by Job Category			
Employees	%	Blue Collar & Service Workers	Office & Clerical	Professional Technical & Sales	Cfficial & Manager
White Males	36.2%	6.2%	36.0%	18.8%	39.0%
White Females	38.1	1.5	87.1	5.6	5.8
Minority Males	8.0	13.1	71.0	7.8	8.1
Minority Females	17.7	1.5	94.9	1.5	2.1

B. Three-Bank Aggregates

B-1) White Males

City	Blue Collar & Service Worker	Office & Clerical	Professional, Technical & Sales	Official & Manager
Atlanta	2.0%	35.1%	17.0%	45.9%
Chicago	6.6	42.0	18.7	32.7
Detroit	8.6	22.6	23.3	45.5
New York	5.8	34.9	19.0	40.3
Philadelphia	8.7	42.4	15.9	33.0
Washington	1.9	40.3	12.7	45.1

B-2) White Females

City	Blue Collar & Service Worker	Office & Clerical	Professional, Technical & Sales	Official & Manager
Atlanta	0.2%	85.7%	8.7%	5.4%
Chicago	4.8	85.8	4.6	4.8
Detroit	1.1	90.7	2.6	5.6
New York	0.4	84.9	7.5	7.2
Philadelphia	2.5	94.0	2.6	0.9
Washington	0.1	90.2	2.6	7.1

B-3) Minority Males

City	Blue Collar & Service Worker	Office & Clerical	Professional, Technical & Sales	Official & Manager
Atlanta	43.5%	52.0%	2.2%	2.3%
Chicago	10.5	71.3	11.4	6.8
Detroit	41.3	37.8	11.7	9.2
New York	5.8	78.3	6.8	9.1
Philadelphia	36.3	47.1	12.9	3.7
Washington	33.7	56.1	4.8	5.4

Note : Few Hispanic Americans are employed in the cities studied, but evidence suggests that males from that group are more likely than females or blacks of either sex to attain upper-echelon jobs. In New York, which has the largest number of Hispanic employees, 10.5% of all Hispanic males are officials and managers and another 4.9% are professionals, technicians, and sales workers. In Chicago, 9.8% are found in each of the two categories. In Washington, 17.1% of all such employees are found in each of the two. The number of Hispanic workers in the other three cities is negligible.

B-4) Minority Females

City	Blue Collar & Service Worker	Office & Clerical	Professional, Technical & Sales	Official & Manager
Atlanta	22.5%	76.9%	0.6%	0.0%
Chicago	1.2	97.0	1.1	0.7
Detroit	0.7	94.7	1.7	2.9
New York	0.3	95.4	1.7	2.6
Philadelphia	3.4	95.8	0.2	0.6
Washington	6.5	91.2	0.9	1.4

C. Individual Reporting Banks

C-1) White Males

Bank	Blue Collar & Service Worker	Office & Clerical	Professional, Technical & Sales	Official & Manager
Chase Manhattan	4.4%	39.2%	22.1%	34.3%
Citizens & Southern	8.3	58.2	5.8	27.7
Continental Illinois	----------------Data Refused-----------------			
First National Bank of Chicago	7.7	35.2	19.5	37.6
First Pennsylvania	6.6	42.9	15.4	35.1
Manufacturers Hanover	7.6	36.1	11.0	45.3
National Bank of Washington	3.2	49.5	---	47.3

C-2) White Females

Bank	Blue Collar & Service Worker	Office & Clerical	Professional, Technical & Sales	Official & Manager
Chase Manhattan	0.5%	87.0%	7.1%	5.4%
Citizens & Southern	0.3	94.6	1.4	3.7
Continental Illinois	----------------Data Refused-----------------			
First National Bank of Chicago	0.1	85.4	7.6	7.1
First Pennsylvania	0.1	97.0	1.4	1.6
Manufacturers Hanover	0.6	82.0	3.9	13.4
National Bank of Washington	0.0	95.0	---	3.3

C-3) Minority Males

Bank	Blue Collar & Service Worker	Office & Clerical	Professional, Technical & Sales	Official & Manager
Chase Manhattan	6.1%	77.0%	10.2%	6.7%
Citizens & Southern	26.1	66.4	5.2	2.3
Continental Illinois	--------------------Data Refused-----------------			
First National Bank of Chicago	5.8	62.7	22.1	9.4
First Pennsylvania	23.2	56.4	9.0	11.4
Manufacturers Hanover	11.0	69.0	10.1	9.9
National Bank of Washington	51.8	45.5	---	2.7

C-4) Minority Females

Bank	Blue Collar & Service Worker	Office & Clerical	Professional, Technical & Sales	Official & Manager
Chase Manhattan	0.3%	96.3%	1.9%	1.5%
Citizens & Southern	11.3	87.4	1.0	0.3
Continental Illinois	--------------------Data Refused-----------------			
First National Bank of Chicago	0.0	96.8	2.2	1.0
First Pennsylvania	1.5	98.0	0.2	0.3
Manufacturers Hanover	0.1	95.7	0.8	3.4
National Bank of Washington	14.1	85.9	---	0.0

Appendix 4

PROBABILITIES*

A. Professional, Technician and Salesworkers

A-1) Three-Bank Aggregates

City	White Male	White Female	Minority Male	Minority Female
Atlanta	1/5	1/11	1/45	1/167
Chicago	1/5	1/22	1/9	1/91
Detroit	1/4	1/38	1/9	1/59
New York	1/5	1/13	1/15	1/59
Philadelphia	1/6	1/38	1/8	1/500
Washington	1/8	1/38	1/21	1/111

A-2) Individual Reporting Banks

Bank	White Male	White Female	Minority Male	Minority Female
Citizens & Southern	1/17	1/71	1/19	1/100
First National Bank of Chicago	1/5	1/13	1/5	1/45
Continental Illinois	------------Not Available------------			
Chase Manhattan	1/5	1/14	1/10	1/53
Manufacturers Hanover	1/9	1/26	1/10	1/125
First Pennsylvania	1/6	1/71	1/11	1/500
National Bank of Washington**	--	----	----	----

B. Office And Clerical

B-1) Three-Bank Aggregates

City	White Male	White Female	Minority Male	Minority Female
Atlanta	1/3	1/1	1/2	1/1
Chicago	1/2	1/1	1/1	1/1
Detroit	1/4	1/1	1/3	1/1
New York	1/3	1/1	1/1	1/1
Philadelphia	1/2	1/1	1/2	1/1
Washington	1/2	1/1	1/2	1/1

* See page 39 for method of calculation.
** National Bank of Washington has no such worker category.

171

B-2) Individual Reporting Banks

Bank	White Male	White Female	Minority Male	Minority Female
Citizens & Southern	1/2	1/1	1/2	1/1
First National Bank of Chicago	1/3	1/1	1/2	1/1
Chase Manhattan	1/3	1/1	1/1	1/1
Manufacturers Hanover	1/3	1/1	1/1	1/1
First Pennsylvania	1/2	1/1	1/2	1/1
National Bank of Washington	1/2	1/1	1/2	1/1

C. Blue Collar and Service Workers

C-1) Three-Bank Aggregates

City	White Male	White Female	Minority Male	Minority Female
Atlanta	1/50	1/500	1/2	1/4
Chicago	1/15	1/21	1/10	1/83
Detroit	1/12	1/91	1/2.	1/43
New York	1/17	1/250	1/17	1/333
Philadelphia	1/11	1/40	1/3	1/29
Washington	1/53	1/1000	1/3	1/15

C-2) Individual Reporting Banks

Bank	White Male	White Female	Minority Male	Minority Female
Citizens & Southern	1/12	1/333	1/4	1/9
First National of Chicago	1/13	1/1000	1/17	zero
Chase Manhattan	1/23	1/200	1/16	1/333
Manufacturers Hanover	1/13	1/167	1/9	1/1000
First Pennsylvania	1/15	1/1000	1/4	1/67
National Bank of Washington	1/31	zero	1/2	1/7

Appendix 5

Council on Economic Priorities Questionnaire

AFFIRMATIVE ACTION

1- When was your EEOC "affirmative action" program adopted?_____

2- How was this policy disseminated throughout your bank and the community?

_____

_____

3- Is your minority employment policy and progress reviewed periodically?_____

4- Have you written an affirmative action program for women? _____If so, how was it disseminated throughout the bank and the community?

_____

_____

5- Have you a program to assist your correspondent banks to set up their own affirmative action programs for minorities? _____ If so, please describe.

_____

_____

_____

6- Are your managers and officers encouraged to serve on boards or as advisors to minority organizations?_____. If so, how many are presently doing so, and in what capacity?

RECRUITMENT, HIRING AND TRAINING

7- Is there someone at your bank responsible for recruiting, hiring, training and upgrading minorities?_____

What is his title?_____

8- Does your bank have a program for recruiting women or

*For proposed modifications of the questionnaire, please refer to p. 177.

minorities at local high schools? _____ If so, please
describe it.

_____

_____

_____

9- Does your bank recruit at colleges?_____ If so, please
indicate on the chart below the extent of this recruitment
effort.

	Total colleges	Total hires	Predom. black colleges	No. of hires	Predom. women's colleges	No. of hires
1969						
1970						
1971						

10- How many people are on your college recruiting team?_____
How many are members of minority groups?_____ How
many are women?_____

11- Does your bank contribute to any MBA graduate programs for
minority or women students?_____ If so, to what
extent?

_____

_____

_____

12- Have your employment tests been validated for minority
groups?_____

13- Have you given any consideration to re-evaluating your
interviewing and testing procedures with a view towards
increasing minority employment?

_____

_____

_____

174

14- Please describe on Chart One any training and upgrading programs for minorities sponsored by the government, the AIB or your bank.

15- Please indicate below how many people have participated in your executive/management trainee program in the last three years.

	Total		Black		SSA (Spanish-surnamed American)		Other minority (specify)	
	Men	Women	Men	Women	Men	Women	Men	Women
1970								
1969								
1968								

16- Please indicate the breakdown of those people hired into the bank at the officer level over the past three years.

	Total		Black		SSA		Other minorities	
	Men	Women	Men	Women	Men	Women	Men	Women
1970								
1969								
1968								

EMPLOYMENT

17- Please complete Chart Two—an expanded version of the EEO-1 form—for the year 1970.

18- Please indicate the number of officers able to commit loans without the authorization of a superior.

Amount of loan	Total		Black		SSA		Other minority (specify)	
	Men	Women	Men	Women	Men	Women	Men	Women
over $1 Mill.								
over $250,000								
over $ 50,000								
over $ 5,000								

175

19- Please indicate how many employees were promoted to officer positions (assistant cashier or above) in the past three years.

	Total		Black		SSA		Other minorities (specify)	
	Men	Women	Men	Women	Men	Women	Men	Women
1970								
1969								
1968								

20- Are any members of your bank's executive committee minority group members?_____ If so, how many?_____ Are any members women?_____ How many?_____

Are any members of your bank's finance committee minority group members?_____ How many?_____ Are any members women?_____ How many?_____

21- Has your bank sponsored any programs or workshops to sensitize employees and supervisors to the problems of minorities?_____ If so, please describe.

_____

_____

_____

_____

22- Have you any such programs dealing with the issues raised by the women's liberation movement?_____ If so, please describe.

_____

_____

_____

_____

176

23- **Does your bank** have formal grievance procedures to handle
employees' alleged discrimination complaints?_____
What is the title of the officer in charge of handling
these complaints?_____

24- **Does your bank** provide employees with any special services,
such as personal counseling, day care facilities, tuition
refund programs, etc.?_____ If so, please describe
the nature and cost of such services.

_____

_____

_____

25- **Does your bank** have any of the following protective restrictions for female employees?

Hours restrictions_____
Weightlifting restrictions_____
Shift choice restrictions_____
Other_____

26- **Does your bank** provide any of the following benefits to
female employees?

Health programs which cover the cost of childbearing_____
Leaves of absence for childbearing_____
Disability benefits for childbearing_____
Retention of seniority during childbearing absences_____

177

CHART ONE

Please describe on the chart below any training and upgrading programs for minorities sponsored by the government, the AIB or your bank.

Type of program and year of contract	Training location (i.e., central office, branches, other)	Type and length of training	Dollar amount of contract	Dollar cost to company	Number of trainees	Number of company hires	Preentry level of trainees	Level of placement after training	Retention rate

178

CHART TWO

Please complete this employment chart for the year 1970.

EEOC CATEGORIES	BREAKDOWN	TOTAL		BLACK		SSA		OTHER MINOR	
		MEN	WOMEN	MEN	WOMEN	MEN	WOMEN	MEN	WOMEN
Officials and Managers	Directors								
	Exec. V-P								
	Sen. V-P								
	V-P								
	Asst V-P								
	Treas'r								
	Asst Treas								
	Cashier								
	Asst Cash								
	Manager								
	Asst Mgr								
	Total								
Professionals	Profess'l								
Technicians	Technic.								
Salesworkers	Saleswork.								
Office and Clerical	Head Tell								
	Sen. Tell								
	Teller								
	Sect'y								
	Clk Typ't								
	Clerk								
	Total								
Craftsmen	Crafts'm								
Operatives	Operat.								
Laborers	Laborer								
Service Workers	Serv Wkr								
	TOTAL								

179

1- Do you have any established program for improving the quality of credit in ghetto areas, eg. direct loans to low-income people, arrangements with department stores which extend credit to the poor, etc.?_____ If so, please describe.

_____

_____

_____

_____

LOANS TO MINORITY BUSINESS

2- Has your bank initiated a lending program specifically designed to make loans to minority businessmen?_____

If so, when was it initiated?_____

What is the title of the loan officer in charge of the program?

_____

3- What were the total value and number of loans dispersed under this program for each year of its operation?

Year	Gross value	Number of loans	Percentage of value guaranteed by SBA or other agency

4- If your bank makes loans to minority businessmen outside of this program, please indicate the value and number of loans dispersed for the same years. (Use chart on next page.)

Year	Gross value	Number of loans	Percentage of value guaranteed by SBA or other agency

5- Please indicate the value and number of conventional loans to business under normal standards for the same years.

Year	Gross value	Number of loans	Percentage of value guaranteed by SBA or other agency

6- What is the nature and extent of management assistance which your bank provides with minority business loans?

_____

_____

_____

_____

7- Does your bank work with any outside organization that provides loans to minority businessmen?_____ If so, please describe your involvement and/or financial and technical assistance.

_____

_____

_____

_____

If the Council were to redesign its questionnaire, CEP would make several modifications.

1.) Question #9, detailing college recruiting efforts, is too vague and misleading as it presently reads. The table should request specific data on the number of employees recruited directly from each college, not all those hired during the year who held college degrees.

2.) Question #16 need not be included in the questionnaire. As banks generally promote from within, rather than hiring from the outside, the question becomes irrelevant to the commercial banking industry.

3.) Question #26, is no longer necessary, as most states have laws which cover this area. Instead, CEP would suggest substituting questions about maternity leave policies, such as when a pregnant woman must commence her leave, if at all, and the duration of that leave permitted by each individual bank.

4.) Finally, CEP would suggest the addition of a question detailing policies and practices surrounding rating, or performance appraisal, systems. The Council found that the fact that an employee sees and signs, or does not, his or her rating is an important factor in evaluating a bank's treatment of its staff.

Bibliography

General

Anderson, Betty R., and Rogers, Martha P. Personnel Testing and Equal Employment Opportunity. Washington, Equal Employment Opportunity Commission, December 1970.

Cross, Theodore Lamont, ed. The Bankers Magazine: A Banking Quarterly Review. Boston, Warren, Gorham and Lamont, Inc.

Equal Employment Opportunity Commission: Reports Numbers 1 & 2, Job Patterns for Minorities and Women in Private Industry. Washington, Equal Employment Opportunity Commission, 1966 (No. 1) and 1967 (No. 2).

Federal Civil Rights Enforcement Effort, A Report of The U.S. Commission on Civil Rights. Washington, U.S. Commission on Civil Rights, 1971.

Harris, Louis & Associates, Inc. The American Public's View of Banks and Bankers in 1970, Parts I and II. Philadelphia, Foundation for Full Service Banks, March 1970.

Hearings Before the U.S. Equal Employment Opportunity Commission on Discrimination in White Collar Employment. New York, Equal Employment Opportunity Commission, January 15-18, 1968.

Industry Wage Survey: Banking, November 1969, Bulletin 1703. Washington, U.S. Department of Labor, Bureau of Labor Statistics, 1971.

Leinsdorf, David, project director. Citibank: A Preliminary Report By the Nader Task Force on First National City Bank. Washington, Center for Study of Responsive Law, 1971.

Manpower Report of the President. Washington, U.S. Department of Labor, Transmitted to the Congress April 1971.

1970 Census of Population: General Social and Economic Characteristics. Washington, U.S. Department of Commerce, Bureau of the Census, Population Division, 1972.

Patman, the Honorable Wright. "Remarks of the Honorable Wright
Patman, Chairman, House Banking and Currency Committee, to
the Public Affairs Forum, Harvard Business School," Monday,
February 9, 1970.

Powers, Thompson, ed. Equal Employment Opportunity: Compliance
and Affirmative Action. New York, National Association of
Manufacturers and Plans For Progress, 1969.

Principles of Bank Operations. no place, American Institute of
Banking, Section American Bankers Association, 1966.

Rogers, Martha P. Employment of Minorities and Women in Commercial
Banking, Research Report No. 32. Washington, Office of Research,
Equal Employment Opportunity Commission, January 1971.

Sawyer, David. "Guidelines - Affirmative Action Program for Banks,
Savings and Loan Associations, and Savings Banks." Washington,
Office of the Secretary of the Treasury, no date.

The American Banker. New York, Published daily by The American
Banker, Inc.

The Federal Civil Rights Enforcement Effort: One Year Later.
Clearinghouse Publication No. 34. Washington, The U.S.
Commission on Civil Rights, November 1971.

Toward A More Viable Financial System, Parts I-IV, "Recommendations
of a Special Committee of the American Bankers Association
Submitted to the Presidential Committee on Financial Structure
and Regulation." February 26, 1971 (Parts I,II) and
May 24, 1971 (Parts III,IV).

Minorities

Corwin, R. David. New Workers in the Banking Industry: A Minority
Report. New York, New York University, Department of
Sociology, 1970.

Patterson, John W. Chicago Area Black Community Banking Opinion/
Usage Study. Chicago, Continental Bank, Marketing Division,
August 1971.

The Job Search of Ghetto Workers, No. 21. New York, U.S. Department
Of Labor, Bureau of Labor Statistics, Middle Atlantic Regional
Office, June 1971.

Thieblot, Armand J.,Jr. The Negro in the Banking Industry.
Philadelphia, University of Pennsylvania, 1970.

Bowman, G.W., Worthy, N.B., and Greyser, S.A. "Are Women Executives People?" in Harvard Business Review. Boston, July-August 1965.

Davis, Susan, ed. The Spokeswoman: An Independent Monthly Newsletter of Women's News. Chicago, Published by Susan Davis.

Equal Employment Opportunity Commission. District Director's Findings of Fact, "Kathleen E. Wells et al. vs. Bank of America, National Trust and Savings Association, Case No. YSF2-050." San Francisco, Equal Employment Opportunity Commission, no date.

Facts About Women's Absenteeism and Labor Turnover. Washington. U.S. Department of Labor, Wage and Labor Standards Administration, Women's Bureau, August 1969.

Fuentes, Sonia Pressman. "Your Rights as a Woman Executive," NABW,Inc. 49th Annual Convention. New Orleans, October 7, 1971.

Hedges, Janice Neipert, "Women Workers and Manpower Demands in the 1970's," Monthly Labor Review. Washington, U.S. Department of Labor, Bureau of Labor Statistics, June 1970.

Koontz, Elizabeth Duncan. "Equality and the Working Woman," Outline of Address Given at a Meeting of the NABW,Inc. of Northern Virginia, October 28, 1970.

NABW Year Book, 1972. Chicago, National Association of Bank-Women, Inc., 1972.

1970 Study of Chicago Career Women. Chicago, Harris Trust and Savings Bank, 1970.

Pressman, Sonia. Job Discrimination and the Black Woman. no place or publisher, March 1970.

Report of A Consultation on Working Women and Day Care Needs. Washington. U.S. Department of Labor, Wage and Labor Standards Administration, Women's Bureau, June 1, 1967.

Rossi, Alice S. Job Discrimination and What Women Can Do About It. Baltimore, 1970.

Stein, Robert L. "The Economic Status of Families Headed by Women," Monthly Labor Review, Reprint 2703. Washington, U.S. Department of Labor, Bureau of Labor Statistics, December 1970.

185

Underutilization of Women Workers. Washington, U.S. Department of
Labor, Workforce Standards Administration, Women's Bureau, 1971.

Womanpower: A Monthly Report on Fair Employment Practices For Women.
Brookline, Mass., Betsy Hogan Associates.

Minority Lending

Bates, Timothy. An Economic Analysis of Lending to Black Businessmen.
Madison,Wisconsin, University of Wisconsin, Social Systems
Research Institute, December 1971.

Brimmer, Andrew F. The Banking System and Urban Economic Development,
"A Paper Presented by Andrew F. Brimmer Before a Joint Session
of the 1968 Annual Meeting of the American Real Estate and Urban
Economic Association and the American Finance Association."
Chicago, December 28, 1968.

Brimmer, Andrew, and Terrell, Henry. "The Economic Potential of
Black Capitalism," Public Policy, Vol. XIX, No. 2, Spring 1971.

Cross, Theodore. Black Capitalism. New York, Atheneum, 1969.

Further Improvements Needed in Administration of the Small Business
Investment Company Program. The Comptroller General of the
United States, July 21, 1971.

Grzywinski, Ronald A. Proposal for an Urban Economic Development
Corporation. No place or publisher, August 1970.

Minority Business Opportunities: A Manual on Opportunities for Small
and Minority Group Businessmen and Professionals in HUD Programs.
Washington, U.S. Department of Housing and Urban Development,
Office of the Assistant Secretary for Equal Opportunity, no date.

Progress of the Minority Business Enterprise Program. Washington,
Maurice Stans, Secretary of Commerce, January 1972.

Rosenbloom, Richard S., and Shank, John K. "Let's Write Off MESBICs,"
Harvard Business Review. Boston, September-October 1970.

Schulte, David M. Banks and Black Capitalism. No place or publisher,
September 1970.